OEDIPUS RETOLD

A double bill:

Oedipus the King

and

Oedipus at the Crossroads

by

Jeremy Kingston

Published by Playdead Press 2014

© Jeremy Kingston

Jeremy Kingston has asserted his rights under the Copyright, Design and Patents Act, 1988, to be identified as the author of this work.

A CIP catalogue record for this book is available from the British Library.

ISBN 978-1-910067-04-8

Caution

All rights whatsoever in this play are strictly reserved and application for performance should be sought through the author before rehearsals begin. No performance may be given unless a license has been obtained.

This book is sold subject to the condition that it shall not by way of trade or otherwise, be lent, resold, hired out, or otherwise circulated without the publisher's prior consent in any form of binding or cover other than that in which it is published and without a similar condition including this condition being imposed on the subsequent purchaser.

Printed by BPUK

Playdead Press
www.playdeadpress.com

Oedipus Retold is a double-bill consisting of *Oedipus the King*, a new adaptation from *Oedipus Tyrannos* by Sophocles, and *Oedipus at the Crossroads*, both written by Jeremy Kingston. ***Oedipus Retold*** premiered at the Tristan Bates Theatre, Covent Garden on January 14th 2014.

Cover Illustration by Paula Lewis

CAST

OEDIPUS THE KING

Oedipus	Tom Shepherd
Kreon	Jack Klaff
Jocasta/Servant	Clare Cameron
Tiresias	Richard Earthy
Shepherd	David Shaw-Parker
Priest/Corinthian	Steve Watts
Citizen 1	Judi Scott
Citizen 2	Luke Hornsby-Smith

OEDIPUS AT THE CROSSROADS

Oedipus	Tom Shepherd
Laius	Jack Klaff
Tiresias	Richard Earthy
Shepherd (Polyphontes)	David Shaw-Parker
Attendant	Luke Hornsby-Smith
Soldier (Chrysippus)	Clare Cameron

CREATIVES

Director   Robert Gillespie
Designer   Faye Bradley
Lighting by   Rob Mills
Stage Manager   Benedict Jones
Casting by   Clare Cameron
Production Consultant   John Nicholls, Arts Quarter
Media Relations   Mobius
Fight Choreography   RC Annie

Author's Note

Oedipus is far and away the best known play surviving from the ancient world and, thanks to Freud, its troubled hero reaches places that other heroes, ancient and modern, do not. Only Hamlet and perhaps Faust come close. Fated since before his birth to kill his father, lie with his mother and beget a brood from which (I quote) the world will shrink in horror, he grows up in ignorance of his doom but upon learning it, within an unspecified number of days – but not many – he has killed a man old enough to be his father and married a recently widowed woman old enough to be his mother. This behaviour struck me as so odd that I wondered if something had been left out of the story.

Sophocles himself leaves inconsistencies in the accounts his characters give of the killing of King Laius and I imagined an encounter between him and Oedipus that does not immediately lead to slaughter but to their discovery of one another's identity. What would happen next?

Sophocles increased the Chorus from twelve to fifteen and in my version of his *Oedipus Tyrannos* I have reduced it to two. This was initially for practical (ie financial) reasons but it enabled me to add what the Greek Chorus may never have done and show them differing among themselves as to how they should respond to what is going on. We no longer live in a time when everyone thinks it desirable to think the same as everyone else, and this is where my version of the Sophocles differs most significantly from the original.

Jeremy Kingston

Director's Note
I vividly recall at the King's Head Theatre, in the 70s working with Joan Crawford (Dan's wife) to discover good scripts. We were on a roll, with a number of successes, and I told Dan I would literally read anything that came in (it was not his favourite pastime). There arrived *Oedipus at the Crossroads* by Jeremy Kingston. Curiously, at that very time I was making notes about an enquiry into the events narrated in *Oedipus Tyrannos* by Sophocles. It had struck me that if the silly fools (his parents) hadn't listened to the Oracle, none of the awful events would have happened; my version would have been in the form of a judicial inquiry, throwing the blame on the staff and operators of the Oracle at Delphi. The length of Jeremy's play made it possible to perform at lunch time and so we had a fair contingent from the RSC in the cast – they happened to be playing nights, in town. Nicky Henson gave us a splendid *Oedipus* and we sold out almost at once.

Immediately, I wanted to put the Sophocles together with Jeremy's sharply comic version of the story. I have had a horror of superstitious religion and its power to wreck people's lives as long as I can remember and so the harmonics between the god-ridden characters of the classic play and the sane, rational *Oedipus* of Kingston's text were irresistible. For years, to mention mounting an ancient Greek drama would cause managers to go white and search for saner company. But things change, so here we are with Jeremy's own translation of the Sophocles to round out a perfect evening.

Robert Gillespie

Cast

Tom Shepherd, Oedipus

Since graduating from Royal Welsh College in 2008, Tom has been working on stage, screen and radio. Theatre credits include playing Kulygin in *Three Sisters*, directed by Elizabeth Freestone, The Director in Terry Hands' *Memory*, Ricardo in *Dog in the Manger*, Mr Barry in *The Lights*, Chase in *Finer Noble Gases* at the Royal Haymarket, Russell in *Dead Pile* as part of Old Vic New Voices, and Sir Charles in *She Stoops to Conquer*, directed by JMK winner Mat Evans. Screen credits include The Storyteller in *Bear Time Stories* (Disney), Mark in feature *My Little Eye* (Dreamcoat), and Mat in *Pleasure Park* (ITV) as well as numerous short films.

Jack Klaff, Kreon/Laius

Jack Klaff is a writer, actor, director and academic whose first movie role was in *Star Wars*. His first television gig - an episode of *The Sweeney* - also featured Morecambe and Wise. And his London stage début, a risqué comedy, led bizarrely to seasons with the Royal Shakespeare Company. Jack has played Walter Raleigh, Bohr, Kafka, DiMaggio, Atahuallpa, Macbeth, Claudius, Iago, Theseus/Oberon, Belch, Trigorin, Gayev, Lord Foppington and a wide range of other parts at prime venues in the UK and abroad. More recently he was Robert the Blind Man in Bill Gaskill's production of *Carver* (Arcola), Michael Mansfield QC in *Stockwell* (Tricycle), Svengali in *Trilby* (Finborough) and John in *Drama at Inish* (Finborough). His films performances have included *For Your Eyes Only*, Jonathan in *King David*, Pasternak in *Pasternak* and Cluseret in *1871*. He has garnered over 200 television credits, including *Vanity Fair*, Ruth Rendell's *Road Rage* and his own works. His latest radio broadcasts have been in Terry Pratchett's *Eric*, the reading of a book about Hugo Chavez, a range of parts in *Dusty Won't Play* and his own play, *Flying Backwards*. He served as a professor at Starlab, a think-tank in Brussels and has held four visiting professorships at Princeton University. He's received two Sony Silver certificates for radio acting, a Tinniswood nomination for new writing, the Jack Hargreaves Award for Innovative TV Drama, two Fringe Firsts, a Herald Archangel Award (2010), a Three Weeks Editors' Choice award and an Ocean Swell medal. (2013)

Clare Cameron, Jocasta/Servant/Soldier (Chrysippus)
Clare is an associate artist, co-producer and casting director for Jane Nightwork Productions. As an actress work includes: Jenny Young in *Denial* (King's Head Theatre), Phoebe Henville in *Someone to Blame* (King's Head Theatre), Marie-Sidonie Cressaux in *Queens of France* (Leatherhead Theatre), Maria in *Love, Question Mark* (Jane Nightwork Productions), The Architect in *Like A Fishbone* (The Cockpit), Corinne in *The Country* (Mountview), Caliban in *The Tempest* (The Cock Tavern), *You've Been A Wonderful Audience* (Baron's Court Theatre), *Macbeth* and *The Taming of the Shrew* (Cambridge Shakespeare Festival), Jane Austen in *Jane Austen Makes a Match* (UK Tour), Christina Rossetti in *Loving Ophelia*

(Pleasance London), Nell Gwynne in *Playhouse Creatures* (The Chapterhouse Theatre). Rehearsed readings include *Useless Mouths* (National Theatre Studio/Jane Nightwork Productions), *Chains* (Trafalgar Studios), *How to be a Good Zimbabwean* (Oval House Theatre), *All Our Yesterdays* (Blue Elephant Theatre). TV and film includes Mary Boleyn in *Henry VIII* (ITV), *The Turing Enigma*, *Cab Hustle* and *Beneath Our Masks*.
www.clarecameron.com
Twitter @1ClareCameron

Richard Earthy, Tiresias
Richard Earthy started his career as the Dauphin in Shaw's *St Joan* at the Lyric Players, Belfast. Seasons include RSC, Stephen Berkoff, Theatr Clwyd and New Victoria Theatre. Credits include Gerald in *An Inspector Calls*, Richard in *Joking Apart*, Herod in *Salome*, Ed in *Sink the Belgrano!*, Ceaucescu in *Moscow Gold*, Uncle Freddy in *Bent*, De Flores in *The Changeling* and Iago in *Othello*. He has performed his one-man show *You Are My Mother* in Edinburgh, London and on tour. Television includes *Lovejoy*, *Grange Hill*, *Shopping and Fucking*, *Big Deal* and *Rockliffe's Follies* (BBC), *Ain't Misbehavin'* (ITV), *Tamar Ben Jelloun* and *Blinded by Light* (Channel 4).

David Shaw-Parker, Shepherd/Shepherd (Polyphontes)
David Shaw-Parker trained at RADA in 1975 and began his career at the Royal Shakespeare Company in 1977 appearing in over twenty five productions between then

and 1991 and returned in 2013 to play The Old Shepherd in *The Winter's Tale*. He has appeared at The National Theatre *in Oedipus Rex, The False Servant* and *My Fair Lady* and in London's West End in *Grand Hotel, The Country Wife, Acorn Antiques, Heavenly Ivy, Up n' Under, A Dead Secret* and *Cyrano de Bergerac*. His numerous television credits include *Inspector Morse, Space Precinct* and *The Commander* and his films include Steven Soderbergh's *Kafka*, Uberto Pasolini's *Still Life* and *The Muppets' Christmas Carol*.

Steve Watts, Priest/Corinthian
Steve was recently in *Relatively Speaking* at the Wyndham's and shortly before that, *Chariots of Fire* at The Gielgud. Other theatre includes: *My Fair Lady* (Theatre Royal, Drury Lane and UK tour, during which Steve took over the role of Henry Higgins), *Jumpers* (NT/Piccadilly), *As You Like It* (Cheek by Jowl, World tour and Albery), *Assassins* (New End, Hampstead), *Pinafore Swing, Mack and Mabel, Plunder, Merrily We Roll Along* and *The Wind in the Willows* (all at The Watermill, Newbury), *The Great Gatsby* (European tour), *Cabaret* (Queen's, Hornchurch), *Into The Woods* (Theatre Royal, York), *Baggage* (Pentameters, Hampstead), *A Christmas Carol* (Vasa, Stockholm), *Beauty and the Beast* (Swan, Worcester), *Enter The Guardsman* (Broadway Bound, QE2) and *Pickwick* (Haymarket, Basingstoke). Steve was proud to be a member of the company at The Open Air Theatre, Regents Park for artistic director Ian Talbot's final season.

Productions there included: *A Midsummer Night's Dream, Lady Be Good, Macbeth* and *The Boyfriend*.

Judi Scott, Citizen 1
Theatre: Madame Arcati in *Blithe Spirit* (Hever Theatre Festival), Mother/Narrator in *I Caught Crabs In Walberswick* (High Tide Festival), Middie Paradock/Mrs. Brandywine in *Absurdia* (Donmar Warehouse), Irina in *Ana In Love* (Hackney Empire), Mother/Adona in *The Romans In Britain* (Crucible Theatre, Sheffield), Ruth in *Map Of The Heart* (Salisbury Playhouse), Hermiane in *The Dispute* (RSC and Lyric Hammersmith - winner of The Barclays Best Theatre Production Award), the title role in *The Mai* (Tricycle Theatre), Tanya in *Tolstoy* (Plymouth Theatre Royal, tour and Aldwych Theatre), Katrin in *The Europeans*, Verdun in *Ego In Arcadia*, The Duchess of Devonshire in *Victory* (all Howard Barker plays for The Wrestling School), Miss Giddens in *The Innocents* (Greenwich Theatre), Eva in *Absurd Person Singular* (Salisbury Playhouse), Lizzie Borden in *Blood Relations* (Old Red Lion), Natasha in *Two Sisters (Waiting For Maria)* a play written by Judith and performed at the Gate Theatre and the Edinburgh Festival, Ben in *Madonna In Slag City* (The Sadista Sisters at the Oval), The Interrogator in *Watching Waiters* (London and Edinburgh), Megan in *84 Charing Cross Road* (Great Eastern Stage).
TV: *Eastenders, Holby City, Picking Up The Pieces, Road Rage* (Inspector Wexford Stories), *Midsomer Murders, Between The Lines, Castles, The Bill, Rides, Missing Persons, Boon*.

TV Film: *Evita's Revenge* (ffpnewMedia), *A Landing On The Sun* and *Bliss* (BBC Screen Two), *News Hounds* (BBC Screen One – Bafta for best single drama), *Tell Me That You Love Me* (BBC Screen Two – winner of the Cannes Fipa D'Or Best Actress Award 1992). Film: *Untitled '13* (Mike Leigh) *Vera Drake* (Mike Leigh – Best Film Award Venice, Evening Standard, British Independent Film), *My Brother Tom* (Dom Rotheroe, Film Four), *Milk* (William Brookfield, Gummfluh Films), *Virtual Sexuality* (Nick Hurran), *High Hopes* (Mike Leigh – winner of the Peter Sellars Best Comedy, Evening Standard Award).

Luke Hornsby-Smith, Citizen 2/Attendant
Luke Hornsby-Smith is an exciting young actor who has trained internationally with Bernard Hiller. His performance in *The Tempest* at the Edinburgh Fringe (Squeaky Door, 2012) received stand-out reviews, and he was selected by the Actors' Guild of Great Britain for their showcase this year. Luke is also a talented vocalist, musician and dancer.

Creative Team

Jeremy Kingston, Playwright

Jeremy Kingston was born in London and brought up in various Home Counties before returning to live in London. Two of his stage plays have been performed in the West End and more on the Fringe, most recently *Making Dickie Happy*, revived at the Tristan Bates Theatre in 2013, and *Oedipus at the Crossroads*, now performed in this double bill with *Oedipus the King*, his version of the Sophocles original. He is the author of a novel *Love Among the Unicorns* and two children's books. For ten years he was the theatre critic of *Punch* and for twenty five years a theatre critic on *The Times*. His first poetry collection *On the Lookout* appeared in 2008 and his second *Who is he, Who am I, Who are they?* in 2014.

Robert Gillespie, Director

Robert is mainly associated with new writing as director. At the founding of the King's Head Theatre he contributed seventeen productions, most of them world premières; as was the production of Kingston's *Making Dickie Happy* at the Rosemary Branch theatre. A play about female gladiators by Debbie Cook and a first experiment at joining Sophocles with Kingston's biting re-write of the Oedipus story also saw first light at the Rosemary Branch. He has contributed shows to six Dublin Theatre Festivals and worked in Israel on, amongst other plays, Frayn's *Noises Off*.

Robert is probably best known as a TV sit-com actor, and starred as Dudley Rush, a part written for him by Brian Cooke, in five series of *Keep it in the Family* for Thames Television. He's also been in everything from *Likely Lads* to *Butterflies* to *Liver Birds* to *Dad's Army* to *Rising Damp* to *Porridge* to *George And Mildred* and he appeared as Gilbert Herring in *Bonjour La Classe*. He featured in Cardboard Citizens' striking production of their WWII epic – *Mincemeat* and was recently seen as Massimo Gentile in *New Tricks*.

As a writer Robert contributed to TV's *That Was The Week That Was*; especially *A Consumer's Guide To Religion* (performed by David Frost) which provoked a fulminating clergyman and questions in the House. Latterly, he has performed in his own two-hander *My Heart* (about death and gods) and directed *Love, Question Mark*, his piece about the myth of monogamy. *Portia*, his solo text for an actress, was played at the recent Women in the Arts Festival at the Tristan Bates Theatre.

Robert is the founder of Jane Nightwork Productions; to keep up with their work, please go to www.janenightwork.com or follow on Twitter: @JaneNightwork

Faye Bradley, Set and Costume Designer
Faye completed an M.A. in Theatre Design at The Bristol Old Vic Theatre School. She was a finalist for the Linbury

Prize for stage design. She recently worked as Trainee Designer for ENO. She was nominated for an Off West End Award for her costume designs for *Fulfil Me Fully Phil*.

She designed *Festen*, at The Space, *The Anorak* at The Lion and Unicorn Theatre *TRASH*, at The White Bear, *4.48 Psychosis* at The Drayton Theatre, *Silent Prayer of Poetry* at The Edinburgh Fringe, *The Yalta Game* at The Alma Tavern Theatre, the set for *The Good Soul of Szechuan* at The Bristol Old Vic Studio and the costumes for *Time and The Conways* at Circomedia.

Faye has a B.A in Fine Art from the University of Leeds, including a year studying in Arizona. She specialised in ceramic and glass sculpture.

After she graduated Faye moved to Japan. She was greatly inspired by traditional Japanese theatre and architecture.
www.fayebradleydesign.com

Rob Mills, Lighting Designer

Working principally in theatre and opera, Rob's work also covers corporate and live events.

Recents Credits as Lighting Designer include: *Gay's the Word* (Jermyn St & Finborough), *Tosca* (UK Touring & Luxembourg National Cultural Centre), *Napoleon Noir* (Shaw Theatre), *Gilbert is Dead* (Hoxton Hall), *Romeo & Juliet* (Cambridge Arts Theatre), *Love Bites* (Leatherhead Theatre), *Curtains* (Landor), *The Elixir of Love* (Stanley Hall Opera), *The Lion the Witch and the Wardrobe* and *Hayton on Homicide* (Edinburgh), *Niceties* (Cambridge Footlights).

As Production & Lighting Designer work includes: *Aida* (Epsom Playhouse), *Madama Butterfly* (Harlequin Theatre), *Venus & Adonis, Dido & Aeneas and The Magic Flute* (Upstairs at the Gatehouse), *The Mikado and Yeomen of the Guard* (Minack Theatre), *The Mikado* (Cambridge Arts Theatre), *Don Giovanni & Pelléas et Mélisande* (West Rd Concert Hall, *Crave* (Edinburgh).

Rob has also provided the lighting & event design for a number of live and corporate events, including the 2010 'Floating Finale' to the Lord Mayor's Show, on the River Thames. He is the founder of bespoke event design company Light Motif. www.robwmills.co.uk

Benedict Jones, Stage Manager

Benedict Jones trained at the Bristol Old Vic Theatre School, graduating in Stage Management in 2013. Whilst there he specialised in stage managing touring shows, including the school's Nativity Tour *Starry Night* and the West Country Tour *Moonfleet*. He has worked on stage management teams for *Dancing At Lughnasa* at the Tobacco Factory Theatre, *A Taste of Honey* at the Sheffield Crucible, and *Surrealissimo* and *Mr Kolpert* at the Alma Tavern Theatre. As well as this he has production managed the Bristol and London transfers of *Disco Pigs*, also at the Tristan Bates Theatre, and recently completed the short tour of *Three Witches* for the Belgrade Theatre and Hoopla Productions. Benedict is looking forward to tackling the thrills and challenges in bringing a show such as *Oedipus Retold* to the stage.

John Nicholls at Arts Quarter, Production Consultant
John founded Arts Quarter in 2008. He has some 25 years' experience of working within the arts, wider charitable communities and creative industries in the UK and overseas.

At AQ, he has overall responsibility for the strategic direction of the partnership in addition to managing the firm's research programmes. John also works with a wide range of clients across all areas of the firm's core business areas as well as developing its learning and professional development programmes.

In addition to serving as Managing Partner of AQ, John is a Governor of Trinity Laban Conservatoire of Music & Dance and a Trustee of South East Dance, where he is also Chair of the Development Committee. In the past, he has served as a Trustee of National AIDS Trust, Headlong Theatre and Campaign for Drawing and was Chair of Pacitti Company. He also acts as ad-hoc advisor to a range of other arts organisations at Board level. John has worked with Jane Nightwork Productions since 2011.

For more information visit www.artsquarter.co.uk or follow John and the team on Twitter @ArtsQuarter.

Tristan Bates Theatre

A 70-seat studio theatre in central London, the Tristan Bates Theatre has a reputation for supporting and showcasing new writing, contemporary productions and work by regional and international companies. The venue offers an ideal destination for audiences in the heart of the West End and Covent Garden, alongside having strong industry connections through the Actors Centre.

The Tristan Bates Theatre as part of the Actors Centre has a vision to support actors, artists and companies not just to achieve the best possible work, but to develop on to the next stages of their careers. Programme highlights in 2012 included the acclaimed European premiere of musical *The Last Session* starring Darren Day; Nirjay Mahindru's *Golgotha* directed by Iqbal Khan (*Broken Glass*, Tricycle/West End; RSC's *Much Ado*); and DYSPLA, the UK's Festival of work by dyslexic storymakers. The building's patrons are David Harewood MBE, Joely Richardson and Rafe Spall.

www.tristanbatestheatre.co.uk

The *Oedipus Retold* team would like to thank, Ben Monks, Will Young, the Actors Centre, Paul Warrington at TCE Creative, Elliot Robinson at Playdead Press, Reverend Martin McGonigle, Claire Lllewellyn and RC Annie.

With special thanks to John Nicholls and Greg Jameson.

OEDIPUS THE KING

after OEDIPUS TYRANNOS by SOPHOCLES

OEDIPUS

PRIEST

KREON

JOCASTA

TEIRESIAS

CORINTHIAN

SHEPHERD

SERVANT

CITIZEN 1

CITIZEN 2

The palace of King Oedipus in Thebes. An altar.
PRIEST at the altar.

Distant chanting.

OEDIPUS enters from the palace

OEDIPUS
I have heard such sounds of grief rising
from the city, terrible grief,
and the signs of it are everywhere.
Offerings. Incense.
But now – and I am glad to see this –
you have come to me, your king,
your Oedipus, to share with me those
horrors you have seen.
Tell me, reverend sir,
speak from your heart to mine.
You must know from
all I have achieved in the past
there is nothing I will not do for
our great, stricken city.
How could I not! Your king!
Speak.

PRIEST
Great king.
Throughout the city, in the market place,
at the temple of Athene, before altars and

shrines here and outside our seven-gated walls,
your people pray to the gods to have
pity on us.
The streams and wells are running dry.
A disease we have never seen before
blights the fruit trees.
Our cattle are giving birth to dead calves,
and not just some do this —
all of them.
Women too, after horrible labour,
their babies are dying or already dead.
And none of us, man or woman, young and old,
are spared the burning arrows of the Plague that is
tearing homes apart, destroying whole families.
    We are praying to the gods, and I,
a priest of almighty Zeus, have come to you.
Not to pray as though you were a god
but because we know you to be
first among men. First among men.
You came to us as a stranger when the
murderous Sphinx was destroying our menfolk.
you answered her riddle and saved our city.
We made you our king, you married our widowed queen
and have guided Thebes wisely and boldly.
Now it is the foremost power in the land.
    So, great king, we implore you
once again to end our despair.
Use your great wisdom, your boldness,
your power and understanding,
to save your people.

Let not the legacy of your reign be
disaster. An empty city.
A ghost ship sailing the wastes of the sea,
her mast broken, her sail rotten,
skeletons her crew.

OEDIPUS
Thank you. Your words are timely.
This scourge unparalleled
which has brought such grief to us –
And I say 'to us' because
while those in the city grieve for themselves I
grieve for all. I, Oedipus,
suffer the pain of thousands.
I have thought long and carefully about
what should be done,
how could this new riddle be solved.
At last I hit on what has to be the wisest course
and have already sent to the Oracle at Delphi
Kreon, my wife's brother,
who is dear to me, honourable
and trusted by all.
He will learn from Apollo what I must do
to save our city. Trust me.
And I am surprised he is not already back.
But when he does come, whatever the god
tells us we must do
I will see it is done, to the letter.

PRIEST
Those men are signalling. Yes,
The Lord Kreon has returned.

OEDIPUS
Oh, Lord Apollo,
Far-darting Phoebus of the Golden Locks!
Let it be good news he brings with him,
words that will open the way ahead
like a piercing eye!

PRIEST
He is smiling!
He comes garlanded with flowers!

OEDIPUS
A good omen.
Welcome home, brother! What message do you bring
from the God?

KREON enters

KREON
The best. And even the hardest task
if we bring it to success inspires us far more fruitfully
than swift objectives easily achieved.

OEDIPUS
Yes... But what is the task?
What words did the Oracle speak?

KREON
Shall we go in to the palace?

OEDIPUS
No. What the god has said
is not for our ears alone.

KREON
Through the mouth of the Oracle the
Lord Apollo declares that an unclean thing
dwells in this land.
It must be found, named and expelled from us.
No other remedy.

OEDIPUS
What manner of unclean thing?
Unclean thing?

KREON
A killer who lives unpunished.
For so long as he does so
the land stays polluted.

OEDIPUS
Who has this killer killed?

KREON
Laius.
King Laius, your predecessor.

OEDIPUS
A crime so long ago.
Before I came here.

KREON
Nonetheless a crime, and the
god tells us, commands us,
to pursue the killer, or killers.

OEDIPUS
Then we shall. But so ancient a crime,
the murderers surely will have fled
and be living who knows where,
unsuspected of this wickedness.
Killing your king.

KREON
The god said clearly we are to search here,
in Thebes. The task may be hard
but the god will ask of us nothing we
cannot do.

OEDIPUS
So. First tell me did King Laius die
here, in the city, outside the city or abroad?

KREON
He left to consult the Oracle at Delphi
and never returned.

OEDIPUS
Did anyone return? His bodyguard?
A servant?

KREON
Only one did so. I remember him,
too terrified to say anything except —

OEDIPUS
Well? What?

KREON
— that a crowd of robbers set upon them,
in a narrow road.
Not one, he insisted, but an armed band.

OEDIPUS
How could anyone dare to do this?
Unless it was a plot,
and they were paid to kill him.

KREON
That thought occurred to us but
we couldn't pursue it.

OEDIPUS
Not even when your king,
your king,
had been murdered?
What could have stopped you?

KREON
The Sphinx. There, on Mount Phicium,
so close, tempting the bravest of our young men to
outwit her. So many failed
and were killed by her, and devoured.
That was a horror greater even than the death of our king.

OEDIPUS
Very well. I solved the Sphinx's riddle and I shall
solve this. The Case of the Death of King Laius
is re-opened. Or opened for the first time.
The god demands it and we obey.
And if killers think they have got away with it once
they will think it worth trying again.
Simple self-preservation urges me on.
      Let us begin. All the people of Thebes must
know what has begun – a search that with the
help of the gods we shall finish.
One way or another.

PRIEST
My thanks, and the thanks of all who will
hear of this new beginning – and a happy end
to follow. Great is Apollo
who sends us warning and guidance
to a better life.

> *OEDIPUS and KREON exit*
> *The PRIEST also exits*

Two CITIZENS enter

CITIZENS
We have heard that a messenger has come
But not what he brings.
The god's oracle will not have been dumb,
her words HIS words, words from the god's own tongue
of what has been done, what has to be done,
they are here, echoing
in the ears of our king.

We must wait, wait to hear, wait to be told.
Mighty Zeus, forgive us!
Our fathers honoured you, trusted you, called
your name and obeyed. We must have failed
and we don't know how. Help us to know! Lord,
look down on us! Save us!
Favour us! Save us!

Bright-eyed Athene, bring to our city
wisdom, justice and peace.
Artemis, ever virgin, take pity.
Golden Apollo, the high and mighty!
Hearken unto us in our frailty!
Bestow on us mercy!
Let our misery cease!

Lastly Dionysos, Lord of the Dance,
Child of Thebes, hear us!
In our ignorance we have given offence.

Show us the road, O Lord, to make amends!
Bend us, O Lord, to what the god demands!
Son of Zeus, be near us!
Lord of the world, spare us!

OEDIPUS enters

OEDIPUS
In the lives of all of us
there come times
when the course we have to take
is uncertain. The issues clouded.
The consequence of this or that decision
far from clear.
But other times occur when
not one iota of a doubt troubles us,
no cloud impedes our vision,
we know what we must do.
Follow me in the decisions I have taken
and the sickness that has long oppressed us will
lift and vanish.

I came, a stranger to this city, after the
crime was committed.
But in marrying your queen I have become
a Theban, joined to the royal family of
the man whose death we mourn.
So
as a Theban I speak to all Thebans:
if any of you know who killed

Laius, son of Labdacus, let him come forward.
He has nothing to fear.
Even if he himself committed the deed
he must leave this land, an exile, but
apart from that, he will go unharmed.

He waits for a reply; none comes.

Then, if anyone among you
knows who the murderer is, a stranger perhaps,
come here from another country,
let him speak. I shall reward him.
And more – I shall be grateful.
The gratitude of princes can transform a life.

Again he pauses; again there is no reply.

But
if one who knows the murderer stays silent,
because he is a friend or relative, the
anger of a prince can also transform a life.
I command that no one shall speak to him,
shelter him, trade with him,
share with him in making sacrifices or
in praying to the gods. Drive him out from
where he has taken refuge, for this same man
keeps the land polluted.
The god has told me this.

Now for the murderer. My curse is upon him.

Whether he did this deed on his own
or in the company of others, let his life now be
unceasing torment, misery and shame.
Let each day of grief be the length of a year.
If he were to be sheltering in my own house
and I knowing of his crime, these same curses
shall fall upon me.

Now that you know what is to be done
let it be done. For my sake, for the god's,
and for the sake of this stricken land where
water fails, crops wither and no man knows
if he will be dead by daybreak.
You should have acted at the start, Sphinx or no.
The death of a king is not some
petty business to be deferred so that
young men can wander off to answer riddles.
But now I wield the power that once he did,
My queen was his queen, his marriage bed now mine.
If their marriage had brought children into this world
those children and mine would have shared one mother.
It was not to be. But I shall fight for him
as though he were my father, and shall not stop
till the killer of Laius, son of kings,
is brought into the light.

Again, my curse upon those who do nothing,
but you, my friends, who know these actions are right,
may Justice and the gods be with us always.

CITIZEN 1
My lord, after such a curse who can doubt
the killers will soon be found.
No, I wasn't one of them. I don't know
who they are, and I'm sure I don't know
anyone who might know.

CITIZEN 2
Apollo knows.

CITIZEN 1
Yes.

CITIZEN 2
Let him be asked to name them.

CITIZEN 1
All-seeing Apollo knows.

OEDIPUS
We can't say why he has chosen to leave the
solving of this riddle to us. One thing is clear:
we can't demand of a god that
he speak more clearly, please,
we didn't quite catch exactly
what you were on about. Sir.

CITIZEN 2
Then, a second suggestion –

OEDIPUS
Make it three, six, a dozen!
All thoughts are welcome.

CITIZEN 2
Of all mankind the lord Tiresias
sees through Apollo's eyes.
Let him be asked to tell us what he knows.

OEDIPUS
Well said, well thought, and done by me already.
The lord Kreon suggested that same course of action.
I have sent for the man, twice. He will be here.

CITIZEN 1
That's good. Otherwise
we only have old rumours to go on.

OEDIPUS
Rumours?

CITIZEN 1
That he was killed, on the road, by –
by – people who surprised him.

OEDIPUS
It is the names we need.

CITIZEN 1
And after hearing your curse they'll be terrified.
they'll come forward.

OEDIPUS
The man who won't shrink at a crime
won't shrink at a curse.

CITIZEN 2
Here is the man you sent for.
The Gods who took away his natural sight
gave him the art that looks beyond sight.
Prophecy. Wisdom. The truth.

TIRESIAS enters, led.

OEDIPUS
Tiresias, you know more
about the doings of this world,
visible and invisible,
than we shall ever know.
I have asked you to share your knowledge of
the curse that lies upon this land.
Who else can we turn to! Who else
(other than those who brought about the calamity)
can reveal their names?
Apollo tells us we must discover
who killed King Laius,
execute them or drive them from the land.

Whatever means you employ to know the
answer to such mysteries I,
Oedipus,
ask you to do this. For all our sakes,
and the sake of the city where, long ago,
you first saw the light of day.

TIRESIAS
(turning) Boy, take me home.

OEDIPUS
What's this?

TIRESIAS
I should not have come. If I had known
why you wanted me here I would not have come.

OEDIPUS
Wait —

TIRESIAS
I should have remembered what you were bound to ask.
The future will be better — but how can it be? —
Yet it may be — if you let me leave, now.

OEDIPUS
I do not grant your request.
Your words suggest you know
something
and will not tell us. That is not the act of a man whose

function is to mark out the future for those who
do not have your very particular in-sight.

TIRESIAS
Oedipus, do not ask me to tell you
more. I will not say more.

OEDIPUS
You mean, though you know the answer,
the cause, the cure, you will not tell us?
To save your – what? – feelings you would
see the city destroyed.

TIRESIAS
Take it how you will. I shall not speak.

OEDIPUS
By the Gods you shall! Or – !
Sir, have I not spoken clearly enough for
      you?
Are you perhaps, as some old men become,
troubled a little in the hearing department?
Or are you just a stubborn, surly, pig-headed,
evil-tempered, old blind bigot?

TIRESIAS
Rage how you like. You will regret it later.

OEDIPUS
You will regret it now!

Anyone who knows the killers,
or anything about them, and refuses to tell
us, his fellow citizens, I have cursed.
And it is all too clear that you have
a very particular knowledge. What if you were a
partner in this crime? Plotted it, ordered it,
even, could you only see, been eager to
commit it?

TIRESIAS
You say that you have cursed him?
You have cursed yourself.

OEDIPUS
What?
What madness is this? Are you unaware
of who I am?

TIRESIAS
Fully aware. Why else should I have said
what I have said?

OEDIPUS
Repeat it.

TIRESIAS
Did you not hear me clearly?

OEDIPUS
Just so that all can hear.

TIRESIAS
You are the murderer you seek.

OEDIPUS
Did you all hear? Shall we call his insults
mere sedition? Actual treason? Or
the ravings of a crazed old man whose words
were taken once as coming from On High,
and now discovers he has lived too long and
no one notices him?

TIRESIAS
Let me tell you another On-High-sent truth.

OEDIPUS
Rave on, old groper.

TIRESIAS
The life that you and the
mother of your offspring have enjoyed is
an insult to the Gods and must be punished.

OEDIPUS
Stop! You've vomited enough filth.
Do you think you can insult the queen
and not be whipped? Gagged? Buried?

TIRESIAS
Truth cannot be buried,

OEDIPUS
Ha!

TIRESIAS
It steals forth, however heavy the
lies that lie upon it.

OEDIPUS
You know nothing about the truth.
Blind, tottering, you have forgotten
how the world must be ruled, even how its people
live. Pathetic.

TIRESIAS
It is sad to hear you use the words
others will shortly use of you.

OEDIPUS
Oh, the dark you live in is a blessing for us.
You can do us no harm

TIRESIAS
I was never the man destined to bring about your fall.

OEDIPUS
Kreon. Of course. How obvious!

TIRESIAS
Not Kreon but yourself...

OEDIPUS
This is how it always goes.
The man who has power, leads his people,
proves skilful in doing so, deals with setbacks
that would defeat his rivals, earns
– rightfully – the gratitude of those he leads,
always there are some men so famished by envy
they will stop at nothing to pull him down.
Did I ask to become king of Thebes?
I was a prince already, prince of Corinth,
but the crown was offered to me, urged upon me.
And now Kreon, in whom I placed my
utter trust, he – what? – sends this witch-doctor
to plot against me. Someone who has proved himself
useless at solving mysteries.
Was it he helped you overturn the Sphinx?
Was it buggery!
A monster, sent by some god presumably,
asking a riddle no one could answer,
and everyone who failed is chewed up –
Shriek, shriek – howls of pain,
mothers in tears, wives widowed,
children left fatherless.
Just the sort of crisis *that* man should have given you
some sort of clue how to solve.
Did he? He said fuck all. I,
Oedipus,
unhelped by any God, any prophecy, any witch-doctor's
abba-jabba, solved it at once.
And it is I, to whom you offered the crown,

that Kreon and this creep plot to replace.
You hope to stand by the throne and satisfy your
lust for power. Well, you and the lord Kreon
will soon learn how painful it is to
plot against your rightful king.

CITIZEN 1
May I suggest that both your words
and the prophet's have been spoken in the
heat of this painful moment. Really,
it isn't that we need, just now.

CITIZEN 2
How do we rid ourselves of the present curse?

TIRESIAS
You may be king and ruler here but I, Oedipus,
do not need to be decorated with gold
trumpery to be your equal in argument.
I am not your slave but the servant of
great Apollo. And I tell you,
you, who sneer at my blindness, that
while you have eyes you do not see
the knots you are tied in, where you live
or who you live with. You don't hear
your father's curse, your mother's shriek of horror.
Now you think you see. When you do see
you will be in the dark. You will cry on
Mount Cithaeron, howl and whimper,
when you learn into whose arms you have been welcomed.

There'll be grief for your children. Blast away
at myself and Kreon. None shall be
so blasted as yourself.

OEDIPUS
Has he done? Get
out of my sight.
Back to your hole.

TIRESIAS
I left it only because you sent for me.

OEDIPUS
I wouldn't have if I'd known you'd stink the air
with your garbage.

TIRESIAS
Is that what you know?
If we could ask your parents
there'd be a different story.

OEDIPUS
What? What do you know about them?

TIRESIAS
Today will bring them to you.
your beginning and your end.

OEDIPUS
My what? You dress your rubbish up in riddles
to pretend there's something fancy in there.

TIRESIAS
But aren't you the expert in solving riddles?

OEDIPUS
Sneer if you will. It has brought me where I am.

TIRESIAS
To your ruin.

OEDIPUS
Away. We have wasted enough time with you.
More than enough.

TIRESIAS
I am ready to go. I have said what you brought me to say
and once again I say it.

OEDIPUS
Enough. Enough. Enough.

OEDIPUS exits to the palace.

TIRESIAS
The man you are searching for, with edicts and curses,
the man who murdered Laius,
is here. A stranger but not a stranger.

Come from his homeland, to his homeland.
and a foul welcome to greet him.
He shall wander over lands he cannot see,
groping his way.

He taps his white stick

He will discover he is brother to his children,
son to his wife,
killer of his father.
Think on that, Corinthian, and when I am proved wrong
then call me the voice of lies and madness.
Away.

TIRESIAS is led away.

CITIZEN 1
The God tells us that someone has –

CITIZEN 2
One man.

CITIZEN 1
Yes. – done these fearful deeds.
He cannot escape Apollo's anger!
His darts of vengeance, divine outrage at such
bold, bloody, bold,
incestuous –
Those darts of vengeance.
And the Furies, sweeping after him.

There's no escape.
The god told us to drive him out
and we will, we have to.
Drive him out.
Over the mountains. Rivers. The sea.
Footsore. Weary. Trying to escape the
relentless pursuers.
But he can't.
And who can doubt this when
it is wise Tiresias tells us so.
But he also said – did I hear him? –
that our king – did he say this? –
is the man he seeks.
The murderer.

CITIZEN 2
What reason to do so?
Corinth has no argument with Thebes.
Their citizens are free to travel here,
ours to go there.
I've never heard of a dispute between
our kings and King Polybus of Corinth.
Nothing I've picked up elsewhere
suggests our King Oedipus could have
brought himself to do what *he* accuses him of.

CITIZEN 1
Nor I. The man who saved us from the Sphinx –
no. He earned the crown we gave him.
I too would have been angered if

he had accused me of any such
frightful thing.

CITIZEN 2
The gods know what men do —

CITIZEN 1
We trust them to. They know.

CITIZEN 2
But even in Delphi they must speak through
mortal tongues.
The Oracle, inspired from On High,
is a mortal woman. He, Tiresias —

CITIZEN 1
— a mortal man.
Mistakes can be made.

CITIZEN 2
This is so.

CITIZEN 1
He's wise, very wise, as wise or wiser than
King Oedipus but mortal.

CITIZEN 2
Certainly.

CITIZEN 1
And just as certain is it that I,
who have known Oedipus since he came here,
watched him, shared in his triumphs
seen the good as well as — well —

CITIZEN 2
The hasty.

CITIZEN 1
At times.
Knowing him as I do I do not,
shall not, can not believe him guilty of these crimes.

KREON enters

KREON
I am told
that our king Oedipus has just now
publicly accused me of plotting,
or actually committing, treason against him.
Yes?
You. Yes?
Nothing is worse than to have such words trumpeted,
and to have them said now, when our city is in such peril!
To be called a traitor!
Is this what he said?

CITIZEN 1
I believe, well, we did hear perhaps —

CITIZEN 2
He spoke those words.

CITIZEN 1
But without thinking properly.
One sometimes does – doesn't think what one's saying.
Words slip out. And to be taken up on them
isn't always what was intended. Necessarily.
On the whole.

KREON
So he has said – let me get this right – that I
persuaded Tiresias to tell lies?

CITIZEN 2
Yes.

KREON
About who killed King Laius?

CITIZEN 1
But as I said, without thinking. I'm sure.

KREON
You mean he just blurted it out once and then talked
of something else and forgot to take the words back?

CITIZEN 2
(shakes head)

KREON
Deliberately he has accused me. I understand.

CITIZEN 1
It's hard for us always to be quite sure of the
ins and outs of high policy –

CITIZEN 2
Here comes the King.

OEDIPUS enters

OEDIPUS
And look who's appeared!
Smiling his honest face.
Can someone have told him he's been rumbled.
His nasty little plot to snatch the throne?
Isn't this the time usurpers always choose to
try their luck? Catastrophe.
Plague. Defeat in war.
The citizens uncertain. What's gone wrong?
That's when the strong man comes forward.
'I can put an end to what's wrong!
Take me for your leader!'
You must think me so very stupid.
And idle.
And ignorant of what goes on inside men's thick heads.
Well, this is no defeat. I have already found
why we are cursed. You.
Get out.

KREON
Gladly, if I were guilty as charged
by you. How should I then stay!
What future could I have,
known to be a traitor, known to have told
lies against you, our king, our leader, our great man.

OEDIPUS
You're clever.
Is he not? The loyalty, oozing with it.
The little sponge of flattery at the end.
It's too late to try that game.

KREON
Just listen to me –

OEDIPUS
Not if you pretend to be innocent.

KREON
Please. Use the clear, bright mind you have been
so famous for.

OEDIPUS
Have been? Did I hear a 'have been' sneak in?
You'll soon find out whether I'm no longer what I was.
If you think being my wife's brother will save you
you've really lost it.

KREON
I would not want to be saved that way. But what is it you claim I've done?

OEDIPUS
Did you or did you not suggest I send for our famous prophet?

KREON
Certainly I did. Who better to advise us?

OEDIPUS
Who better, eh? Right. So how long is it since my predecessor...

KREON
Your predecessor?

OEDIPUS
...met his end.
Murdered. Assassinated.

KREON
Many years, alas. Before you came to us.

OEDIPUS
And was our famous prophet famous then?

KREON
Of course.

OEDIPUS
And mentioned me, did he?

KREON
Not that I remember.

OEDIPUS
You did try to find out who killed your king?

KREON
As I said before, we did all we could at the time.

OEDIPUS
And the great reader of matters hidden from us lesser men,
he pointed his stick at no one?
Why not?

KREON
I can't say.
I don't know, and I won't try to guess.

OEDIPUS
But I think you do know and I won't guess.
Your first move was to bring him here,
foaming at the mouth, to point to me and screech,
'There is the guilty man!'

KREON
He says this?

OEDIPUS
How innocent the guilty look!

KREON
Till this moment I had no idea
he had accused you.

OEDIPUS
Had you not?

KREON
Believe me.

OEDIPUS
Believe a man who for years has dreamed and
schemed to take my place?
Who takes advantage of our present
terrible danger to spread the wickedest lie?
Who could believe you?

KREON
Listen and you must believe.

OEDIPUS
Must?
See how smoothly the 'must' slips in!

KREON
I ask you to listen. I hope you will believe.

OEDIPUS
Nothing you can say will make
a charge of murder stick to me.

KREON
You are married to my sister.

OEDIPUS
Is that a question? Yes, brother-in-law Kreon,
I am husband to your father's daughter Jocasta.

KREON
And in ruling this land you share power
equally with the queen?

OEDIPUS
It is the custom.

KREON
And I have always been equal with the two of you
in power.

OEDIPUS
Making your treachery the more vile.

KREON
Think about this power of mine.
It gives me what I want.
It gives me all I want.
I don't aim for and never have aimed to be hailed as King.

What more would that bring me – except the power to
    exile *you!*
Uneasy lies the head of a king, on his golden pillow:
I sleep well at nights, on
my golden pillow.
Why ever should I swap the one for the other!
King Kreon? No. But Kreon, brother-in-law to King
    Oedipus?
Oh yes. Indeed yes.
People greet me. Salute me.
If *he* were to want some favour from you
very likely he'd come first to me, knowing
I've always found you ready to grant my
occasional requests.
What's in it for me, what would I gain
from your downfall?
Your disgrace?
Your replacement by one who does not
want what you possess?
If you still can't accept this is the truth I'm telling
go yourself to Delphi, with or without me,
repeat to them the message I brought back,
check that I told it correctly.
And if – though it's inconceivable –
you find I have plotted with the wise,
the rightly famous Tiresias,
yes, execute me. There –
I'd sentence myself if this was a crime I'd committed.
But I'd want proof. And you must have proof.
Not this wild,

panicky
suspicion. I don't understand where it comes from,
why you should suddenly
fix on the innocent.
Thinking a bad man good is stupid, and dangerous,
but thinking a good man bad is worse than that: it's
  unjust.
And without justice, stern, precise justice,
uncovering what has been done,
seeing errors for what they are –
deceits, delusions, gaps of memory so
smoothly covered we fail to see the gap –
turn aside from treating every man justly
and it's a dark world we'll be heading back to,
dark and dangerous and a bad time to be alive.

CITIZEN 1
That's good advice, my lord. Surely it's better,
I'd have thought,
to be cautious than too quick.

OEDIPUS
And when the assassin is quick, what then?
I hold my hand out and his knife's in my throat.
He speaks of his innocence.
But then he would, wouldn't he?

KREON
What is it, brother, you want of me?

OEDIPUS
Guess my answer.

KREON
Banishment?

OEDIPUS
No. I want to see the knife go into your throat.
I want you dead.

KREON
Oedipus.
A madness has taken possession of you.

OEDIPUS
Not of me it hasn't. I see clearly enough.
A traitor. A liar. A man who's
wanted to thrust me out for years. Planned it,
plotted – that's what I see.

KREON
What can have happened! When the city needs
wise decisions –

OEDIPUS
Aha! The strong man slithers forward.
I rule here.

KREON
And if you rule badly?

OEDIPUS
You hear him? All that garbage about
'I don't want to be King,
I just want to stroll about and do favours for everyone – '

KREON
I want the city strong and safe and well.

OEDIPUS
And I do not? This is my city.

KREON
Mine too.

OEDIPUS
Not for much longer.

KREON
Mine since birth!

OEDIPUS
And now death!

CITIZEN 1
My Lords, please –

CITIZEN 2
Lords, the Queen must have heard you
and is here. For all our sakes
end this perilous quarrel.

JOCASTA enters

JOCASTA
What are you two fools doing!
shouting, screaming, you can be heard
in the depths of the palace!
At a time like this, people dying,
you bicker like street kids.

KREON
Sister, your husband is in such difficulty.
Shall he banish me or slit my throat!

JOCASTA
What's this?

OEDIPUS
He speaks the truth there, for a change.
I have found him out, plotting to kill me, plotting
to grab the throne.

KREON
The gods be my witness!
Never have I even thought of doing that!
Never.
By the gods.

JOCASTA
Believe him, Oedipus.

He cannot be lying.
And for my sake, the city's sake.

CITIZEN 1
Believe him, Lord.

OEDIPUS
What?

CITIZEN 2
No one has ever doubted his word,
his loyalty –

CITIZEN 1
His honour.

CITIZEN 2
His love for the city.
And now he has sworn by the high gods
he tells you the truth.

OEDIPUS
You ask me to believe him?

CITIZEN 1
He has sworn it.

CITIZEN 2
And where – my Lord – is the proof
against him?

OEDIPUS
So you want me dead? Booted out?

CITIZEN 1
No, Lord!
By the Sun, greatest of Gods,
may it go dark for all time
if ever I'd want such a thing!
May friends, children, the gods themselves
abandon me!

CITIZEN 2
But here, now,
when the whole land is suffering,
still suffering,
patch up your quarrel. Sir.

OEDIPUS
I can't stick a patch on
an open wound
as wide as this land.
It's my life or his.
But so be it. Guilty though he is,
He keeps his life, vile though it is.
Go. Go.

KREON
I see something bad in you that I've
not seen before. Never thought to see, ever.
I don't like to think what's behind it,

nor what it heralds for the good
governing of our country.

OEDIPUS
Just get out of my sight.

KREON
Your command is my wish.
Thank you, good citizens,
for your belief in me.
Sister.

KREON exits.

CITIZEN 2
Madam, we would understand if you
and the King wished to withdraw.

CITIZEN 1
At this juncture.

JOCASTA
In good time. First,
what has been happening?

CITIZEN 2
Words, ma'am, words.

CITIZEN 1
But even words meant innocently
can be at times upsetting.

JOCASTA
Words from both?

CITIZEN 2
From both.

JOCASTA
Saying what?

CITIZEN 2
Today's situation is so delicate,
and those who are given
the honour of steering the ship of state must consider
so many issues – better, I think, to leave
preliminary stages of discussion
preliminary.

OEDIPUS
Now you see what your meddling has done.
Slanting decisions it is not for
such as you to take.

CITIZEN 1
My Lord –

CITIZEN 2
Nothing would make us dare to interpose,
still less to go against, the wise orders
of a wise helmsman of our ship.

CITIZEN 1
Steer us again as you did before
safely into safe harbour.

JOCASTA
Oedipus, tell me what has happened.
You're still furious. You hunch your shoulders when
your temper rages all over the place.

OEDIPUS
I have good reason. And *I'll* tell you.
They'll get it all wrong.
Kreon began it.

JOCASTA
What did he begin?

OEDIPUS
I killed the King – he says.

JOCASTA
Dear Gods! To your face?

OEDIPUS
Oh, no. His mouthpiece is that stinking prophet.

Your brother wants to keep himself Lord Squeaky Clean.
The prophet prophesied some prophetical prophecy.
I killed the king and therefore
down I must come.

JOCASTA
Forget it.
There's no such thing as prophecy.
Drop this and I can tell you
confidently it will hit the ground.
But doomy forecasts of distant crimes
far far into the future… Rubbish.
And I'll tell you what made me think so.
Soon after I married Laius an oracle came.
Not from Apollo himself directly: brought by
one of his priests.
Fate had decreed that Laius was to be killed
by a son he fathered and that
I would bear.
Our son would kill him.
Well, to prevent that, when a son was born
Laius bound his ankles and had him exposed
on some mountain.
And as everyone knows Laius was in fact killed
by robbers at a place where three roads meet.
So the prophecy that our son would kill him
just didn't happen.
So much for prophecy.
I say wait for the gods to undrape the future
as we walk into it.

OEDIPUS
Something you said –
Something you said back there reminds me...

JOCASTA
Yes?

OEDIPUS
Wait.
You said he was killed at a crossroads
where three roads meet?

JOCASTA
That's where it happened, they say.

OEDIPUS
And where is this crossroads
where it happened?

JOCASTA
On the road to Delphi. A third road joins it,
somewhere in Phocis.

OEDIPUS
When?

JOCASTA
The actual day I couldn't tell you
but news reached us
shortly before your victory over the Sphinx.

OEDIPUS
Oh. Oh.
What have I done!

JOCASTA
You're frightening me. What's this about?

OEDIPUS
Tell me – King Laius – describe him.

JOCASTA
Middle-aged, middle height, dark hair but
greying. Otherwise, not unlike you.
As you might become in time.

OEDIPUS
Have I called down on myself
my own curse?

JOCASTA
What do you mean? What is all this?

OEDIPUS
Suppose the prophet did see the truth...
Just one thing more.

JOCASTA
Anything if it'll make things better.

OEDIPUS
Was Laius travelling with a large guard
proper to a king, or lightly attended?

JOCASTA
Something in between. There were five, I think,
Yes. A herald, three guards, Laius in his chariot.

OEDIPUS
Oh. All too clear.
Who brought the news?

JOCASTA
The one guard who escaped.

OEDIPUS
And what happened to him?

JOCASTA
He stayed here a while, recovering,
and then – about the time you came – he
asked me, begged me, to send him back to his
former work in the fields and pastures.
He wanted to be as far away as possible from the city.
I agreed. He had done a good service.

OEDIPUS
He is alive? Can he be brought here?

JOCASTA
I daresay but why?

OEDIPUS
We have only to open our mouths,
the tongue's cage,
and it runs wild, snapping at anything.
I'll keep the bars locked, I think.

JOCASTA
Won't you just tell me a scrap of what
started you off on all this
horrid fear. I hate seeing you
suffer like this. Please.

OEDIPUS
Very well. Listen.
I grew up, as everyone knows, in Corinth.
My father the king, mother the queen, myself the heir.
Nothing to worry about.
Cloudless days. Until the night
a man stinking of drink staggered up to me
and sneered that I was not the king's son.
I knocked him down. Of course.
And questioned my mother and my father
who were outraged and the man was punished but
these things niggle. They niggled me.
At last I left home, telling no one, leaving behind
friends, everything I knew.
I went to Delphi.

I needed the Oracle to tell me if that drunk
knew something about me that I did not.
But the Oracle said nothing about my past.
Only my future interested her, and that's a murky story.
I'm to marry and fuck my mother,
there'll be children and – beforehand, I suppose –
I kill my father.
So, I've not been back to Corinth since.
Risk killing my parents?
Any life anywhere was better than having
that kind of sometime turn into my now.
I left Delphi and I
came to this place that sounds too much like
the crossroads where your husband died.
There – I'll tell you just what happened –
a herald, and some men around a chariot,
and a middle-aged brute in it.
I call him brute with reason.
First he shouted at his herald,
"Push him off the road!" Me. The herald tried
and failed. I knocked him down,
and a guard or two, and then the old man
leaned from his chariot and with his
horse-prod jabbed me here.
You're wrong. I don't have a temper.
But when insulted or attacked,
by anyone, I know what to do.
I knocked him out of the chariot,
killed him, killed the others.
But if he was King Laius I've done

something so reckless cursing the killer.
And I've – I'm – I'm the polluting,
unclean thing that must be driven out.
It's not the curse I uttered: it's the crime.
I killed your husband and took you in his place.
Oh.
Where do I go? Not back to Corinth,
to kill my father, marry my –
It's your husband's fault.
He's had his revenge. He's laughing somewhere.
(to CITIZENS)
Happy now? It's Thebes's problem solved.
Apollo will be pleased. Mission accomplished.
Fly back up to Zeus. "Well done, that god."

CITIZEN 1
My lord, what you tell us does sound alarming but
if the man who brought the news gives his account
in his own words all may be well.

OEDIPUS
Maybe. Where does he work now, this one-time guard?

JOCASTA
He is a shepherd.

OEDIPUS
If his story tallies with what you said
I may be saved.

JOCASTA
What did I say?

OEDIPUS
Robbers killed him. Robbers. Not one man.
And if he still says so I'm in the clear.
But if it turns out to be one man on his own
I'm not.

JOCASTA
He can't change now what he said then.
The whole city heard him.
Even if he does there's still Apollo's Oracle
quite wrong.
Laius was to die at the hands of his son.
And did he? Could he have?
A son left to die on a mountainside
one week old?
I tell you, from the day my husband died
I wouldn't cross the road for an Oracle
or give a prophet the time of day.

OEDIPUS
You may be right. Still,
send someone for this shepherd.

JOCASTA
I'll do it now. Come.
We'll have you smiling again
In next to no time.

OEDIPUS and JOCASTA exit to the palace

CITIZEN 1
I hope
that all I have done
and will do
keeps obediently to the laws
laid down for us by the gods.
The immortal gods, visible, invisible,
there, beyond the clouds of
Mount Olympus.

CITIZEN 2
And likewise that all I say,
have said and will say
has kept and shall keep
to the law.

CITIZEN 1
It is not mortal man who laid out
rules of behaviour, how men should deal with men,
with women, in home and city,
shrine and temple.
The immortal gods decreed those laws.
They must be followed.
We follow the gods.

CITIZEN 2
A man can

believe himself above all laws.
Or be himself the law.
Chance and the nudges of fortune
help him hack out a course to the mountain peak
and fall blinded by a stronger sun.

CITIZEN 1
But – gods on high – don't let
those obliged to follow such a man
follow his fall.
Anyone who – man, or woman – scorns
publicly the gods, outraging those who hear her,
risking our hard-won safety
and peace won by hard effort.
And the gods' blessing always, always –
anyone who does this and still flourishes
in defiance of what is proper,
how can the people then trust the gods?

CITIZEN 2
Why go to Delphi, to Olympia, to any of the
shrines and temples that utter prophesies
if what they say will be certain
fails to occur?

CITIZEN 1
No one will go. Why should they!
Can the gods –

CITIZEN 2
— be deaf to us?

CITIZEN 1
No. Can the gods fail?
No, no, not that. Never that.
The prophesies given to this King Laius, this
King Oedipus, must, however terrible,
be fulfilled.

CITIZEN 2
Or the gods will fail.
And then what?

> *JOCASTA enters, with offerings for the altar*

JOCASTA
I deemed it proper
to come with offerings. The king
is not his proper self.
He listens to nobody, except those
who make him feel worse.
Keeps asking why it should be
he has been singled out.
He can't understand. I can't understand!
But are we meant to understand?
The gods know.
Apollo, great Apollo,
Deeds have been done that defile us.

Our land suffers.
Cleanse us.
Send us what is needed.

CORINTHIAN enters

To end our pain.

CORINTH
Is this the palace of King Oedipus,
can you tell me?
I have good news for him.

CITIZEN 2
This is his palace.
and here you see his Queen.

CITIZEN 1
Wife and the mother of his children.

CORINTH
Greetings, good lady, and may all good things
Come to you and be with you always.

JOCASTA
I thank you.

CORINTH
I bring you good news. And sad news.
One and both together.

JOCASTA
How so? Where are you from?

CORINTH
Corinth.
The citizens want Oedipus to be our king.

JOCASTA
But what of King Polybus?

CORINTH
Dead.

JOCASTA
Dead!

CORINTH
Alas. But are we not mortal?
We are mortal all.

JOCASTA
(to CITIZENS) Go. Tell the king.
Dead!

> *One of the CITIZENS exits to the palace*

You do bring good news.
In all the years my husband has been king here
he dared not return to the city he left.
An idiotic prophesy made him afraid

that he might somehow kill your king.
Yet he died a natural death?

CORINTH
Yes, madam.

JOCASTA
There! Oracles!
Why are we so foolish!

OEDIPUS enters; the CITIZEN follows

OEDIPUS
Why have I been called out here?

JOCASTA
To listen to this man and laugh at prophesies.

OEDIPUS
Who are you? Who is he?

JOCASTA
From Corinth. And he is here to tell you that
King Polybus has reached the end of his life
in your absence.

OEDIPUS
Is this so?

CORINTH
I had thought to tell you of the good news first
but, yes, our queen is now a widow.

OEDIPUS
But how did this happen? Has there been
some violence in Corinth?

CORINTH
No.

OEDIPUS
Illness?

CORINTH
He died in his bed, my lord, yes, but from old age.
He had been king many years when I was still a boy.

OEDIPUS
Ah, my beloved partner. Ha!
Why do we do it? Why do we make these journeys to
that smoking crack in the earth at Delphi?
We watch for birds flying this or that way,
Cringe at thunder-claps.
The folly of us all!
My father's dead and I've not killed him.
Unless – did the Oracle mean
he'd die of grief at never seeing me?
No, even oracles can't be so subtle.
So. I am free.

JOCASTA
As I could have told you.

OEDIPUS
I would not have listened then.

JOCASTA
But now what is there to fear!

OEDIPUS
Ah. I was to marry the one woman
who of all women I must not.

JOCASTA
Forget all that.
Doesn't this prove it's
chance and what we make of it that hurls us
onward through life? Seize opportunities as they come.
As you have done.
What you fear doing with your lady-mother
millions of men have done before you
in their dreams. Dreams —
forget them. That is how to live.

OEDIPUS
Yes. I know. But while she still lives
I can't forget. I have to be afraid
until she's gone.

CORINTH
My Lord? Who is it you fear?

OEDIPUS
Merope. Your Queen. My mother.

CORINTH
May I be so bold to ask why?
She is old and frail.

OEDIPUS
A prophesy, my good fellow. A fearful doom
will follow me if I do such and such.

CORINTH
I stand rebuked. It is not for me
to ask questions of my future king.

OEDIPUS
He does not know that my fame sprang
from my skill at answering questions.
Nor can I see you as being
dangerous as the Sphinx.
The prophesy is that I will take my mother,
old though she is, into my bed
and kill my father.

CORINTH
Is this why you have stayed away from them
for so long, so many years?

OEDIPUS
What other reason would I have?
Not to see one's parents is a great sorrow;
to see them a surpassing joy.

CORINTH
Well, my Lord. I can release you from this fear.

OEDIPUS
You have already done so.
My father is dead.

CORINTH
I can tell you more than this.

OEDIPUS
But you have said the queen still lives.

CORINTH
So she does, sir. So she does.
You will be amazed, I think, by what I have to say.
I won't deny I volunteered to come here
in hope, to be honest, of a reward.

OEDIPUS
Of course. I shall be generous if you can take away
an old and wretched fear.

CORINTH
I can do that. It is because of this prophesy that you have feared to see your parents?

OEDIPUS
I have said so.

CORINTH
King Polybus and Queen Merope?

OEDIPUS
Who else!

CORINTH
Who else…
Of course you would call King Polybus your father.

OEDIPUS
He called me his son.

CORINTH
I have heard him do so.
I was the first to hear him do so.

OEDIPUS
If you have something to say to me
now say it.

CORINTH
King Polybus is no more your father than I am.

OEDIPUS
Take care.

CORINTH
I handed you to him myself.
From my hands into his.

OEDIPUS
What are you saying?

CORINTH
You'll have heard how they longed for a child
and were not blessed with one until you came.

OEDIPUS
I have always known this.

CORINTH
It was I who ended their long longing.

OEDIPUS
Then where am I from?

CORINTH
Not from my house. I found you
in the shade of trees on Mount Cithaeron.

OEDIPUS
That is Theban country.
What brought you there?

CORINTH
I was a shepherd then. In the summer
I took my flocks up to rich pastures
high on the mountain.
And one day there you were, crying.

OEDIPUS
In pain?

CORINTH
Look at your feet, sir.
Through your ankles had been driven a bronze nail.

JOCASTA stares at him

I drew it out. Soon your crying stopped.

OEDIPUS
The scar remains to this day.
Cithaeron.
Then I am Theban born.
A grove of trees my nursery,
Cithaeron my mother. Is that the oracle's meaning?
Who would drive a nail
through a newborn baby's feet?

CORINTH
For the answer to that you'd have to ask
the man who gave you to me.

OEDIPUS
My father?

CORINTH
I think not. No. I am sure not.

OEDIPUS
So who is this next man in my
tangled family thorn bush?

CORINTH
He was another shepherd.

OEDIPUS
Uh-huh. Also from Corinth?

CORINTH
No. From here. His master would have been
King Laius.

OEDIPUS
Is he still alive?

CORINTH
That I can't say.

OEDIPUS
Can't say?

CORINTH
I do not know.

OEDIPUS
(to CITIZENS) Do you, or anyone you know, know
who this shepherd might have been?
Or if he's still alive?
If you don't know I command you to find out.
There have been too many secrets,
too much seen but unsaid
and that stops now.

CITIZEN 1
My Lord, I think he is the man you have already
summoned.

OEDIPUS
(to JOCASTA) You said that before he became Laius's
guard he was a shepherd.

JOCASTA
Yes, but it cannot be him. He won't know.
He'll know nothing.

OEDIPUS
Something he may know. I have to follow this
unexpected twisted trail where it leads me.

JOCASTA
Do not. Oedipus, do not.
There is danger, such danger now.

OEDIPUS
Lady, I will not take it as disgrace
if I am the son of slaves.

JOCASTA
But stop. Just stop.
We do not have to know everything.
We cannot know everything.

OEDIPUS
But this it may be I can know.

JOCASTA
But don't. Don't.
It will be the death of me.

OEDIPUS
Tut. I'll not stop. Go,
if you cannot bear to hear that my father
kept the royal pigs.

JOCASTA
Oh…! Oh…! Oh…!
What has been done…!
By you and to you!
Oh, my abandoned man.

My poor man. Oh…!

JOCASTA exits

CITIZEN 2
What does she mean, Oedipus?

CITIZEN 1
Leaving us, suddenly, in such alarm,
and tears. As though some horror
is about to burst on us.

OEDIPUS
Let it burst! I will know who I am.
She may be ashamed of having allied herself
to the son of a shepherd, or slave,
or criminal –
I say that we make ourselves what we can.
We see what Chance has brought to us
and bend it, ride it, use it, guide it.
Chance brought me this way. I could go no other.
No other life could have been mine but
this one that she and I, Chance and I,
have made together.
Whoever my true father is
Chance has been my true mother.

CITIZEN 1
Privileged are we to be living at this time!
To hear such words, to share this moment!

Citizens, we are led by grandeur.
What other place in all the world
has for its chief one who – I dare to say –
was so mysteriously, propitiously
brought to the world! Cithaeron!

CITIZEN 2
Cithaeron.
In the sacred oak grove on your highest peak
great Zeus wed glorious Hera.
Was it on your flanks, Cithaeron,
that our King Oedipus saw his first dawn light?

CITIZEN 1
Is it the god Pan who fathered you?
Often he is to be seen there.
Or Apollo, golden Apollo?

CITIZEN 2
Shall it be you, Dionysos,
born here in Thebes of our queen Semele
and Zeus?
God of living things, and life itself,
did you come to Cithaeron to
father your own hero?

CITIZEN 1
O! Privileged are we to have been given
life at this time!

OEDIPUS
My friends, we are waiting for a shepherd
to enlighten us further. Could anyone be
more supremely shepherd-like
than this old man?

SHEPHERD enters

Would you say our waiting is at an end?

CITIZEN 1
It is, my Lord. And he is one of the late king's
longest-serving and most trusted men.

OEDIPUS
And you, Corinthian, is this the man you knew?

CORINTH
The very same. I recognised him instantly.
What good fortune that we are both still here
to join our stories!

OEDIPUS
You, old man. Come here.
I have been told you once served King Laius.

SHEPHERD
I did, sir. All my life. A servant to
the last king
and since.

OEDIPUS
What work have you done for us?

SHEPHERD
Mostly caring for sheep, sir. That mostly.

OEDIPUS
Where did you take them for the summer grazing?

SHEPHERD
Always Cithaeron or nearby.

OEDIPUS
This man here – what do you know of him?

SHEPHERD
What do I –? What should I know?

OEDIPUS
Look at him. Have you met before?

SHEPHERD
Not that I remember. But my memory is not good.

CORINTH
Let me speak to him, my lord. I'll make his
memory work again. He won't have forgotten that
for three whole summers I brought my flocks up from
Corinth to Cithaeron where they grazed alongside his.
Three summers, and at the end of each

we'd part and go our two ways.
You remember now?

SHEPHERD
Yes. Yes. It was so long ago.

CORINTH
And you remember when you gave me a child,
a baby. To look after.

SHEPHERD
Never!

CORINTH
Yes. Here is that child! – a man! – your King!

SHEPHERD
Hold your tongue, hold your tongue!

> *SHEPHERD threatens the
> CORINTHIAN with his staff.
> OEDIPUS takes hold of it.*

OEDIPUS
Would you! This'll be across your back
if you won't answer.

SHEPHERD
Answer what, sir, what?

OEDIPUS
Did you give him that child?

SHEPHERD
He's the one whose mind has gone.
He knows nothing.

OEDIPUS
Very well.

> *OEDIPUS snatches the staff, twists the SHEPHERD's arm up behind his back.*

SHEPHERD
No, no! I don't remember.

OEDIPUS
This'll make you.

SHEPHERD
Oh, no!

OEDIPUS
Did you give that man the child?

SHEPHERD
I did. I wish I'd died that day.

OEDIPUS
You'll die today if there's more lying.

SHEPHERD
Oh. Oh.

OEDIPUS
Where did you find the child?
Was it left somewhere? Is it yours?

SHEPHERD
I – not mine. No. I was given it.

OEDIPUS
Given it? By whom?

SHEPHERD
I can't say. Oh! No! Someone
from the house of Laius.

OEDIPUS
A slave? A slave gave it you?

SHEPHERD
(shakes his head mutely)

OEDIPUS
Then who?

SHEPHERD
Why have I not died before today!

OEDIPUS
You'll not die before you speak.

SHEPHERD
I was told
it was the king's child.
The Queen will tell you more.

OEDIPUS
The Queen? She gave it you?

SHEPHERD
Yes, my Lord.

OEDIPUS
For you to do what?

SHEPHERD
To let it die?

OEDIPUS
So it was the King's child by a slave?

SHEPHERD
No, sir. Her own.
There was a prophesy
their child was to kill its parents. I took pity on it
and thought if I gave it to this man he'd take him
far away and the child would not meet its parents.
But if that child

is you, master,
I have saved you from death
for something far more terrible.

OEDIPUS
It is clear at last.
Oh, everything I did to escape this crime
brought me closer to it.
I have asked all that is needed
to know what it is I am.
I'll ask nothing more. I'll see nothing more!
I have been cursed in my birth! Cursed in my marriage!
Cursed in those I killed.
Enough!

> *OEDIPUS exits*
> *CORINTHIAN and SHEPHERD also exit*

CITIZEN 1
We have fallen.
Great Oedipus has fallen who drew us up with him
to the highest peaks. What hope is there
now for us?

CITIZEN 2
What hope for any man, woman, child
treading out the years below the hammer beats
of sun and moon.
Nothing comes of it. Nothing.

CITIZEN 1
Yet what glory was his!
When our young men were each day dying
under the claws and teeth of the
winged, implacable monster,
Oedipus saved us.

CITIZEN 2
Of course we made him our king.

CITIZEN 1
Were we wrong?

CITIZEN 2
Oedipus made us great.

CITIZEN 1
Mighty. Feared. Seven-gated Thebes.

CITIZEN 2
Were we wrong?
Unknown to us this
terrible crime has been
sapping the rock in which we placed our trust.

CITIZEN 1
Unknown to us.

CITIZEN 2
Unknown to us son and father
shared the same warm resort.

CITIZEN 1
Unknown to us.
Unknown to him. To her.

CITIZEN 2
We are told.

CITIZEN 1
Our city will be known not for its glory
but for its shame.

CITIZEN 2
I am no prophet but I can see
Thebes going down into failure and defeat.
wiped off the outraged face of the earth.

CITIZEN 1
You have done this to us, Oedipus.
I wish you had never saved us, if it was
only to lead us into the dark.

SERVANT enters from the palace

SERVANT
What are you doing, citizens of Thebes!
How can you be still

when what has occurred within the palace
must have sent a shudder out to the
farthest sea and mountain.
What grief you will feel when you hear of
deaths arrested, deaths achieved, and the horror.

CITIZEN 1
What more can there be than what we know already?

SERVANT
For one, the queen has hanged herself.

CITIZEN 1
Oh, no –!

CITIZEN 2
Gods –!

SERVANT
She came running across the colonnade
tearing at her hair, her robe, her breasts,
crying out words we could make no sense of.
She ran into the bedchamber and bolted the doors
but now we could hear her crying out to King Laius,
what they had done, what she had done,
and to King Oedipus, what they had done.
After this we heard nothing because
Oedipus had come amongst us
raging, raving, shouting for a sword, calling out
for the queen not by name or rank but by a word

for a place from which not only his children but
he himself had issued.
'Where is she? Where is she?' he cried but
none of us dared tell him.
Yet perhaps he knew, or was directed by some god,
because he reached the chamber doors and
threw himself against them.
How he could do so I don't know but the bolts bent back
and he fell into the room. Us behind him.
Then we saw the queen, hanging, turning.
With a roar he sprang up to untie the knot,
laid her carefully on the floor but all life was gone from her.
But then something far worse. So much worse.
He tore off the two brooches fastening her robe and
dug the pins into his eyes.
Crying out – I don't know – they had seen what they
should never have seen, and would now
see nothing more.
Over and over again he jabbed the points into his eyeballs.
Blood soaked his cheeks and then
a black hail of blood spurted out.
In so short a time has the joy they shared
plummeted to grief, ruin, shame and death.

CITIZEN 2
Where is… the king? Where is he now?

SERVANT
He was shouting that he must come out here,
to be seen by all the city, his father's killer,

his mother's — no, I can't say it.
He says he must leave the city, leave our land
and take his curse with him.
Here he comes!

Enter OEDIPUS, blinded

CITIZEN 1
I can't look! How could you have done that!
How could anyone blot out the world
deliberately! Did a god force your hand?

OEDIPUS
I'm outside. Am I? Am I? Am I?
I have left the place — O god! — the place

CITIZEN 1
O, make it not have happened!

OEDIPUS
For ever in the dark, forever and forever.
But there are no nails to put a stop to thought!
Where to end that knowing who I am!

CITIZEN 1
No man can put an end to his thinking
this side of death. If this is what you tried for
it was not wisdom, my lord.

OEDIPUS
I hear your voice. I sense you – there?
Are you there? And you – there?

CITIZEN 2
We are here.
We too have to learn what has happened to us
in what has happened to you.
And why it should have ended this way.
in blindness.

OEDIPUS
Would you have had these look upon
anything, having seen so much!
What is there in the width of the whole world that,
seeing it, could bring me peace or pleasure?
Every tree will tell me of Mount Cithaeron
where I should have perished.
Every living animal speak of the sheep guarded
by men who so fatally guarded me.
Every man will be the father whose life I put an end to,
every woman my shamefully treated mother.
every child my own sons, my daughters,
who are my brothers, my sisters.
Tell me after that
what good I should find in sight?

CITIZEN 1
We understand.

CITIZEN 2
Yet
in saving yourself from seeing us
you have stopped us seeing you.
Our suffering is nothing like yours.
What could be greater than
what you have undergone. Yet
we ask ourselves
as citizens
what are we to make of
this calamity, so long in growing,
ripening and bursting upon us all?
We might have come to learn of you
what was done wrong at the start of things.
But now your blindness
bludgeons us into ignorance.

OEDIPUS
The Gods in their cruel wisdom know
why things are as they are.
(to CITIZEN 1) You, friend,
take me from here, lead me to the city gates
to make my way out of the land
polluted by my presence.

CITIZEN 1
I will do so. What vengeance
the Lord Apollo has meted out upon you!

OEDIPUS
But I did this! My own hands
dug out my eyes!
I curse the man who pulled the nails from my feet
and forced the life on me that leads me here.
Cithaeron should have vomited me forth
rather than let me lie on her.
Corinth, what a perfect, sweet, honeyed life
I led there – a false skin
masking the horrors gathering within.
And then, to the narrow road, hemmed in by trees,
where three roads meet, and Laius meets
his murdering son.
And here, where even worse is done.
I am guilty in my ignorance
because the gods will it so.

CITIZEN 2
But how are we to take their verdict, Oedipus?
You must tell us.

OEDIPUS
Obediently.
You want to question what I have done,
I know it.
Best to speak briefly of vile things.
and I have spoken enough. Take me
anywhere. Kill me. Throw me from some high crag
into the sea. Take my hand – No!
Put your hand here. Do you dare to touch me?

CITIZEN 2
For what you want done you must ask the Lord Kreon.
He will have to steer us now into our future, guide
across the monster-haunted seas
our damaged ship. In him we must place
trust again, hoping

KREON enters

Here he is.

OEDIPUS
Here? No. What can I say to him?
I abused his trust, accused him of treachery.
I was wrong, altogether wrong.

KREON
I have not come to mock you, Oedipus,
or to rake over the past.

(to CITIZENS)

You have not acted well in keeping him
here for all to stare at.
Apollo has told us this is an unclean thing,
an affront to decency, to the earth, to the
sun that must see all.
Take him into the palace. Only kinsmen
should see such an obscenity.

OEDIPUS
I hear your words gladly. You know what I am.
Do one thing for me. It will not be for my sake but yours.

KREON
What are you demanding?

OEDIPUS
Fling me out of this land, now, now.
Get me to some place where no man goes,
where I can perish.

KREON
That I would have done already, I assure you.
But the god must advise us.

OEDIPUS
We know what the god wants!
He ordered us to find my father's killer
and thrust me out like the filth I am.

KREON
You remember his words well, contributing
something of your own. But
so shocking is the outcome to decent eyes,
and so many errors, such disobediences have
occurred, it is wiser to ask afresh.

OEDIPUS
You will be asking what to do about me?

KREON
That is exactly what we shall ask.
And this time, I trust, you will obey.

OEDIPUS
Without question.
No more questioning.
Bury my wife, my mother, your sister,
in whatever manner, with what solemnity
you feel appropriate. Ha! Appropriate!
Ask Apollo not to retract his
earlier judgement. I cannot stay
here. Let me go to
Cithaeron, where my father and your sister,
wanting me dead, fixed on to be my tomb.
Let it be so. There I'll die.
I could not have died there the first time,
wanted as I was for this
discovery, this
lesson for the world.
That is what and all I am:
instruction.
As for my children, Kreon,
the boys will become men. They will
hack out lives for themselves. The girls
will find a grimmer future. Who will want to
ally himself to a family where the father
is their brother. Look after them,
my lord.

KREON
I will of course be doing so.

OEDIPUS
May I hold them, once more,
so that I take with me a last memory
of how we once were —
at peace, we thought,
happy, we thought,
with the years ahead spreading before us
like a wide plain to build the future on.

> *The two daughters of OEDIPUS appear from the palace*

I hear something. I hear crying.
Have you brought them out
for me to touch one last time?

KREON
I have done so.
Come. Face your wounded father.

OEDIPUS
Where are you, children?
Closer. Ah.
These eyes see nothing but my hands can tell me
which of you, yes, is which.
There is so much I looked forward to telling you,
so much I would tell you now.

How you should bear yourself in a life that will be
thorny with hardship.
How, when happiness comes, you should not
trust it. Why should it last?
Why should any good last when so much that is
rotten surrounds it?

KREON
Enough. You have said all you need.
Go back to the palace.

OEDIPUS
So soon. On one condition.

KREON
Say what this condition is.

OEDIPUS
That you send me swiftly out of it,
out of the city, out of this land I once ruled

KREON
No. That must wait on the god's word.

OEDIPUS
But since he hates me –

KREON
When the god speaks, then you will be told
what is to become of you.

OEDIPUS
You will keep to that?

KREON
I am not in the habit of saying
what is untrue, nor of undertaking
courses of action I do not propose to complete.

OEDIPUS
Then I obey.

KREON
Let go of the children.

OEDIPUS
Not yet. Let them go with me.

KREON
It is not appropriate.
Let go of him.
You are no longer king. And do not rule but,
as you have said, obey.
Once you were king here, once you steered us
to these rocks. Let go.

> *OEDIPUS lets go of the children*
> *All exit except CITIZENS, who now face us*

CITIZEN 1
And so, people of our great city,

look and learn, look and be taught.
First, think on Oedipus's fall and pity
him who had been magnificent now brought
lower than the blind moles that crawl
beneath our feet,
who are not cursed with recollecting all
they once possessed, gloried in, found sweet
before the fall.

CITIZEN 2
The lesson is that – that we are – that we are nought.
Yes, that must be it. All that we have thought
was ours to achieve, or understand, or simply do,
brings in the long run – and the short run too –
little to be happy with, of little worth.
That's the reward for being on this earth.
Oedipus's will is free: he chooses
to ask his questions and he loses.
And yet, faintly I sense a different way
to wisdom, though I –

CITIZEN 1
                Secondly: obey!
Our Gods are mighty. In this life of woe
that's all we know on earth and all we need to know.

Black

End of play.

OEDIPUS AT THE CROSSROADS

OEDIPUS

SHEPHERD (POLYPHONTES)

SOLDIER (CHRYSIPPUS)

LAIUS

TIRESIAS

ATTENDANT

A rock.

A signpost pointing in three directions: Thebes, Corinth, Delphi.

A fat sheep.

OEDIPUS walks on from Corinth.

OEDIPUS My name is Oedipus. My father is King Polybus of Corinth and my mother is Queen Merope of Corinth. *(waits)* I see you've heard the rumours. Nobody told me the rumours, of course. I have to wait till that loudmouth Deliboeus staggers over to me at dinner last week and says, "Hey, Fatfoot — !" My friends call me Fatfoot on account of my swollen ankles. "Fatfoot," he says, "how come you have such big swollen ankles when your ma and pa both have thin dainty ones?"

Well, I'm quite a dab hand at riddles but I was pretty drunk myself and couldn't work out the answer to that one. So I said, quick as a flash, "If your father has the stomach of a pig and your mother has the face of a cow, how come you have the brains of a crab?" Not bad for the spur of the moment.

But he went on about my ankles and their ankles and my curly hair and their straight hair... Well, you know the rumours: I'm not really King Polybus's son but only adopted; an old shepherd found me when I was a week old, abandoned on a mountain; the King and Queen brought me up as their own son because they hadn't any of their own.

It's not a story that has the ring of conviction.

For instance, how did they convince everyone I was their son? In Corinth everyone gossips about everyone else all the time. A chambermaid gets pregnant down by the harbour and next morning they're talking about it right up in the citadel. I just can't see the Queen being able to come out onto the palace steps one fine day and say, "By the way, I forgot to mention it but I've been expecting a baby this past nine months and here he is.

Anyway, I'm on my way to consult the Delphic Oracle to find out the truth. Not that I believe in oracles. I don't. But people go to Delphi with their problems from all over the world. All the cities keep agents there. And the temple priests run a highly efficient intelligence system. Glimpses into the future...? *(shakes head)* But facts about the past and present... *(nods)* You never know: that shepherd who's supposed to have rescued me from the mountain could have gone to the Oracle to find out what he ought to do with me.

SHEPHERD walks on from Thebes.

Good day, old man. How long will it take me to get from here to Delphi?

SHEPHERD   You'll be making for the Oracle?

OEDIPUS   I may drop in on her while I'm there.

SHEPHERD   Two days till you see the spray rising from the waterfall between the two cliffs. Another two hours and you reach the first temple on the Sacred Way.

OEDIPUS   You speak as though you have been there yourself.
I said you speak as one who knows the place.
Tell me what I may expect.

SHEPHERD   The priests will tell you that.

OEDIPUS   Shepherds in this part of the world are noted for the lovable gruffness of their speech.

SHEPHERD   I'm not from these parts. Don't you think that. I keep my flock on
Mount Cithaeron, twenty miles yonder. Only come down this part of the world lambing time. *(sees sheep)* There you are, beauty. How many are you going to give us this year? *(feels sheep's belly)* Two? Three? Come on with you

SHEPHERD walks off with sheep towards Corinth.

OEDIPUS   Mount Cithaeron belongs to the city of Thebes. King Laius and Queen Jocasta. Nasty goings-on they have there. Wouldn't surprise me if that shepherd could tell a tale or two. Right.

OEDIPUS walks off towards Delphi.

Black.
Newborn lamb cries.
Light.
Rock. Signpost.
A thin sheep and a black lamb alongside.

OEDIPUS walks on from Delphi.

OEDIPUS   Well. I hardly know how to say it. I'm not sure I want to say it. I've always been fond of my mother. I've always been fond of my father. If he is my father, if she's my mother — the Oracle never got around to dealing with that. It was "Out of this place! Blemish on the face of the earth! Horror of horrors!"

They've chosen the site very cleverly. Mount Parnassus there; and the two lines of cliffs coming together at a right angle by the gorge; and the temples spread out on the slopes below. And there's a mist blowing from the waterfall and creepers dripping down from branches of vast trees. And once you get inside the Sacred City and zigzag up the Sacred Way past the Sacred Rock and the Sacred Tripod to the Sacred Temple there's the ritual washing in the Sacred Spring and the ritual lighting of the ritual torch. And the ritual stunning of the sacrificial ox with the sacred axe and the ritual cutting of its holy throat. And then the ritual disembowelling and the scrutiny of the entrails and finally: the cave underneath the temple and the thing sitting at the end of it.

I don't know if she was a woman or a man or a boy dressed up in rags or what. She looked exceedingly old and horridly thin and drugged. From the smell of the laurel leaves and whatever else was burning I should say she probably spends all her time doped. Which is why she wouldn't want to eat, which is why she's so thin. All I had time to say was, "I am Oedipus" and she began to throw herself about and beat at the fire with her stick and wail and ululate. I thought at first this was part of the usual performance so I stood there waiting. Then when her ululating had died down a bit she pointed a finger at me. Not *at* me, actually, because she was blind or pretending to be. She held her finger out as if pointing at me but in fact over my shoulder. It was rather a good, unnerving touch. *(shrill voice)* "You will live to kill your father. You will lie with your mother and beget children of her."

That surprised me too because I'd understood the Oracle made its pronouncements in neat hexameters. There was nothing neat or hexametrical in what she bawled at me. And the priests were no help either. When I came out of the cave they were all racing away down the hill. What you do when you've consulted the Oracle, you see, is go to the priests and they help you understand what her message means. Usually it's hexametered so ambiguously you need all the help you can get to make any sense of it at all. Perhaps they thought my message was clear enough. I had to drag one of the priests out by his ankles from under a tripod to get him to speak to me. I said, "Look. I came here to find out who my parents are and all your Oracle has said is I'm going to kill one of them and marry the other." He fell down in a heap and begged me not to breathe on him or he'd be defiled. I left him crawling away to wash himself in the sacred brook. I wandered around for a bit banging on the pillars, and just as I was about to leave a youngish sort of priest popped out from behind a tree. And kept out of breath-range. But said he was frightfully sorry for the upset but as far back as anyone could recall the Oracle had never reacted like that. And parricide *was* an awful crime and incest was quite as bad and he hoped I would appreciate, etcetera, etcetera. And if there was anything he could do, smarm, smarm. So I said I'd found out what I came for, thank you. Obviously Polybus and Merope aren't my parents because even if I did accidentally kill him one day it's pretty unlikely I'd follow it up by marrying her. "That being so," I said, "all I need do to keep out of danger and show your precious Oracle up as a fake is take care from now on (a) never to kill any man old enough to be my father. And (b) never to marry any woman old enough to be my mother."

SOLDIER *(off)* Make way! Make way! Make clear the road for the King!

SOLDIER, armed and helmeted, strides on from Thebes.

Get off the road!

OEDIPUS Get off the road yourself.

SOLDIER King Laius of Thebes draws near.

OEDIPUS The road is wide and free from boulders hereabouts. Let him go round me.

SOLDIER attacks OEDIPUS. OEDIPUS draws his sword.

Wait. Let me see your face. Are you old enough to be my father?

SOLDIER laughs, pushes up his helmet. He is in the pride of young manhood.

SOLDIER   Sonny.

SOLDIER lowers his helmet. They battle.
Distant trumpet.
SOLDIER jumps back from OEDIPUS and looks along the road to Thebes.
Horses hooves, chariot wheels approaching.
SOLDIER advances on OEDIPUS and continues the fight.

LAIUS   *(off)* Whoa...!

Horses stop. SOLDIER fights desperately.
LAIUS stalks on from Thebes.

SOLDIER   *(fighting)* He wouldn't step off the road, Sir! He wouldn't get off the road!

LAIUS draws his sword, advances on OEDIPUS.
OEDIPUS detaches himself from SOLDIER, swiftly wounds LAIUS who staggers back against the rock.
OEDIPUS returns to SOLDIER and kills him.
SOLDIER falls to the ground. OEDIPUS returns to LAIUS.

OEDIPUS   I'm sorry, sir, but really you shouldn't have interfered.

LAIUS groans, gestures him away. OEDIPUS examines the wound.
Oh, come now, that's nothing at all.

OEDIPUS spits on the wound, tears strip from LAIUS's robe, bandages wound.

LAIUS   *(faint)* Water . . .

OEDIPUS   I don't think there is any.

OEDIPUS looks around, walks over to sheep, feels under her; walks over to dead SOLDIER and takes off his helmet; returns to sheep, milks her into the helmet and takes it to LAIUS. LAIUS drinks.

LAIUS   Is he dead?

OEDIPUS   I'm afraid he is. And if a young Corinthian may advise an old Theban: If you order your soldiers to say please, they'll live longer.

LAIUS   What is your name, Corinthian?

OEDIPUS   Oedipus. It means Swollen Feet. I have these swollen ankles. My father is Polybus, King of Corinth, and my mother Merope, Queen of Corinth. That's to say,

	I've always understood they were my parents but the Oracle seems to imply otherwise.
LAIUS	I am on my way to the Oracle.
OEDIPUS	Better not tell her you met me. I am a blemish on the face of the earth. My very breath defiles.

LAIUS stands, walks over to the dead SOLDIER, looks down at him. He kneels and kisses his face,

LAIUS	You always said you wanted to die for me…
OEDIPUS	*(embarrassed)* I really am most terribly sorry —
LAIUS	Don't talk to me of your sorrow! What did you know of him! To you he was just a thing with a sword, a creature to be killed — not loved, worshipped, known. *(unseen by OEDIPUS, he takes hold of SOLDIER's sword)* Take him up.

OEDIPUS does so.

He will need a serving-man in the next world.
OEDIPUS, holding SOLDIER in his arms, sees the sword in LAIUS's hand.

OEDIPUS   I am a king's son, not a servant.

LAIUS   So much more the honour to him.

OEDIPUS   Yes. To kill me would be one way to prove the Oracle wrong. The reason I am a thing of horror — in the eyes, the blind eyes, of the Oracle — is that I am destined to kill my father and marry my mother. If you send me into the next world now I shan't have done either so obviously the Oracle no longer works.

Since OEDIPUS's revelation LAIUS has not moved.
OEDIPUS looks at him, puzzled; touches him.
LAIUS's body is rigid.
OEDIPUS puts down the SOLDIER; turns again to rouse LAIUS, knocks away his sword, pinches him.

King Laius?

OEDIPUS turns away uncertainly.

LAIUS speaks, as though in a trance.

LAIUS   Yes, Lord. *(OEDIPUS stares at him)* Lord Apollo. Far-darting Lord whose laws men try to evade but cannot. *(kneels)* Forgive Thy servant who sought to escape Thy curse. Even at this late hour, O Lord, I beseech Thee, forgive me if so it be Thy will.

Pause. LAIUS rises.

Oedi-pus. *(speaks the name reflectively; studies OEDIPUS)*

May I see your swollen ankles.

OEDIPUS removes his sandals.
LAIUS looks at his feet, kneels again and looks at them, bows his head, weeps.

OEDIPUS   Oh, now, look here, please —

LAIUS   Take him out of the sun.

OEDIPUS picks up the dead SOLDIER, looks at LAIUS, carries the body behind the rock.
LAIUS sobs, twice. He stands.

OEDIPUS returns, limping.

LAIUS   You limp.

OEDIPUS   The stones are hot and sharp.

LAIUS   Hotfoot for Corinth, eh. Give my regards to your father.

OEDIPUS   What's so riveting about my ankles? Everywhere I go people want to look at my ankles. When they hear my name their eyes do a quick flick down to my feet to see what's wrong with them. I get in first now. "My name is Oedipus," I say. "It means Swollen Feet." OK, so I have an arthritic condition of the ankle bones. It's a slight deformation. One thing, though: nobody's ever wept over them before. I suppose I'm lucky you didn't ask to see my arse. Oh, word gets around.

LAIUS   You insult me.

OEDIPUS   I criticise you. Sodomy's all very well for recreation but a king's first duty is procreation. I don't know what's the matter with your generation! King Polybus can't have children so he has to adopt me. You spend all your time with sexy boys. Who rules Thebes when you die?

LAIUS   The Queen has a brother, Kreon.

OEDIPUS   I shall rule in Corinth because I am the adopted heir. Unless Polybus *is* my father, and my mother some concubine... I could accidentally kill him — a discus thrown in the air where the wind carries it across the stadium and drops it onto his old grey head. I can see that could happen. If he told me who my mother was I could call on her, greet her, admire her beauty, if she still has beauty, and take care not to marry her. Even if he doesn't remember who she was or where she is... how old would a woman have to be to be my mother? I'm nineteen. Really it shouldn't be difficult to avoid marrying any woman nineteen years older than me! My point is, you see, I recognise how easily, how gradually, how almost without realising it, one could step onto the safe path of not marrying or not having children, to avoid a curse. Some say that's why Polybus and Merope had no children. The Oracle warned them not to. So of course they obeyed. A child would be sent to them, said the Oracle. With swollen

	ankles. Do you know any big-ankled people who lost a baby nineteen years ago?
LAIUS	You mock the Oracle. Yet you went to consult it. If you don't believe in the truths of its prophecy, go abroad. Go away from this part of the world. Far away. Find yourself a place where the people pay no more heed to the Oracle than you do.
OEDIPUS	On my first afternoon at Delphi I met men coming to consult the Oracle from all over Greece. Macedonia. Thrace. Phrygians wearing those floppy red caps. Assyrians with indigo beards. Egyptians. Romans. It would not be possible to find any place in the known world where people do not bow down and grovel before the whims and dictates of that old blind skinny filthy thing squatting in the dirt of her stinking cave.
LAIUS	*(gasps)* Like the young men in Thebes you mock, spit, shit on the Gods. For you nothing is holy, no place sacred. It's all so much antique junk to be tossed about by your mean scabby little minds.

OEDIPUS spreads his feet, holds his arms up to the sky.

OEDIPUS   Far-darting Apollo! Phoebus of the Golden Locks! Pierce me with your arrows, your plagues, your rays of death! Non-existent Lord Apollo, strike!

LAIUS   You blaspheme!

LAIUS makes to knock him down, draws back.
OEDIPUS turns his head to regard him.

OEDIPUS   You can't strike me down. If you killed me you'd prevent me killing my father and Apollo's Oracle would be proved junky. And you had better not maim or disfigure me. I've got to attract my mother, remember, make her demand my services between the incestuous sheets. You can't stop that. Che sera sera.

He lowers his arms, picks up sword, sheathes it.

I wish you joy of your oracle, old man.

OEDIPUS moves off towards Corinth.

LAIUS   Oedipus. *(OEDIPUS turns)* We cannot escape our fate. *(OEDIPUS nods ironically)* Twenty years ago I sent to the Oracle to find out why my Queen bore me no children. The Oracle returned the answer that what I regarded as a curse was a blessing, for if she were to bear me a son he was destined to grow up and kill me. After learning this it was naturally impossible for me to allow myself any further congress with my wife. Nor was it safe to lie with any woman. Hence my regard for young men. But one night the Queen tricked me with drink, came to my bed, aroused me and conceived. From that day she was forbidden, on pain of instant death, ever to come to my bed again. And as soon as the son was born, the son destined to kill me, I seized it from the nurse's hands and had him exposed on Mount Cithaeron. I handed him to one of my shepherds. And lest the babe should crawl his way to safety from the wolves I had his heels pierced and clamped together with an iron nail. He passed out of my life. I had outwitted the Oracle. Who had also prophesied that after killing me my son would lie with his mother and beget children of her.

OEDIPUS is motionless. LAIUS looks at him closely.

Oedipus? Son?

Unlike LAIUS, OEDIPUS is in no trance.

OEDIPUS I'm thinking. Did you enjoy driving the nail through my feet?

LAIUS I can't remember what I felt. Fear. I felt fear. Of a baby ten minutes old.

OEDIPUS In Corinth the babies crawl at six months. Perhaps five months. At ten minutes, never.

LAIUS It was necessary to make sure.

OEDIPUS You could have killed it. Me. Outright. That would have made sure. The mountains all over Greece are dotted with babies exposed by their parents for one reason or another. It's a primitive form of population control. But to hand the babe to an old shepherd... Notoriously prone to tender feelings, old shepherds are. What you felt it 'necessary to make sure' was that I did *not* die. So that somehow someday, grovelling, god-struck little king,

I should come back to kill you; somehow wed your widow. And ready for the day when the questioning began and answers were required, you took care to mark me, specially, here, unmistakably, so that I should always be recognised for who I am and what I had done.

He examines his ankles.

I wonder who took out the nail..?

Behind them a flock of sheep passes from Corinth towards Delphi, followed by SHEPHERD.
OEDIPUS calls him.

You!

SHEPHERD ignores him.

Shepherd!

SHEPHERD walks off towards Delphi.

LAIUS   Polyphontes!

OEDIPUS stares at him.
SHEPHERD returns.

	Are you in the pay of my enemies?
SHEPHERD	No, my lord.
LAIUS	Blind?

SHEPHERD shakes head.
LAIUS points towards Thebes.

	What do you see there?
SHEPHERD	Your gold chariot, my lord, glittering in the sun.
LAIUS	And?
SHEPHERD	Two horses.

LAIUS strikes him across the mouth.

LAIUS	And?
SHEPHERD	The body of your servant.
LAIUS	You still deny you are in the pay of enemies? You see your king alone with a stranger. What's that on his sword? Rust? He has killed my man, he has come to kill me, and you hobble past with your head turned.

SHEPHERD   My Lord, I am a shepherd, an old shepherd. Old in the head. I saw the chariot from across the valley and the horses standing idly between the shafts. My way lay past this place but I hoped to pass by quickly, thinking you and your man might be praying. When I saw his body lying against the rock I knew not what to think. And then I saw the stranger and heard voices raised but — great king — I thought no man would dare raise his sword to you. I thought: a lovers' quarrel. Perhaps the stranger was a kinsman of your man, or you wished to choose the stronger... Had I seen you fighting I would have done what I could. Though an old shepherd... A stick merely...

LAIUS   Was it you drew the nail from his feet?

SHEPHERD looks at LAIUS, at OEDIPUS, at LAIUS; throws himself at LAIUS's feet.
LAIUS holds a sword above SHEPHERD's neck.

SHEPHERD   My lord, I did as you ordered. I carried him that night up the slopes of Mount Cithaeron and left him in a hollow, his feet shackled, no longer bleeding. I thought him dead already. The next morning I returned to the place and he was whimpering. Still alive. I left him again. I moved him into the shade and left him. And when I returned that evening one of my sheep was suckling him. I had left him to die but Fate — Fate who moves us all! — had moved that sheep to keep death from him. I knew not what I should do. But that night the Lord Apollo came to me in a dream. He ordered me to bring my flock and the babe to this very spot, here where three roads cross, and wait for a man like myself to come. I feared to disobey your orders but I dared not disobey the God. After two days waiting a shepherd came up from Corinth and I understood the words of the God. I wondered if you too, my lord, were obeying orders from the God and that the babe was marked out for a high destiny. I gave the babe to the Corinthian and warned him to care for it well for its origins were noble and the Lord Apollo watched over its life.

SHEPHERD looks at OEDIPUS.

OEDIPUS   I expect you'd like to look at my ankles.

SHEPHERD does so.

Thank you, old man, for preserving my life. And the old sheep, if she's alive, who wetnursed me.

SHEPHERD   And the Lord Apollo.

LAIUS   You are right to think the Lord Apollo spoke to me about the babe. Not in a dream but through the Oracle at Delphi, prophesying that when the babe grew to manhood he would kill me, his father.

OEDIPUS   And that's just been confirmed by the Oracle to me. I am to kill him.

SHEPHERD   O Lord Apollo, marvellous and mysterious are Thy ways, proceeding from on high! We mortals crawl upon the earth —

OEDIPUS   Get up, old fool. I don't propose to kill him. The Oracle is false. On the other hand, your king believes the Oracle speaks true. So he won't kill me. As a result: nobody is going to kill anybody. We shall remain here for a while, talking of family matters, then part — I to Corinth, he on to Delphi. That is all.

LAIUS   But should the Oracle prove true, old shepherd, Polyphontes, you would recognise this man again?

SHEPHERD   Yes.

LAIUS   You would recollect the day you took him as a babe, nailed through the ankles, up Mount Cithaeron?

SHEPHERD   Yes.

LAIUS   You would not forget that he met me here?

SHEPHERD   No.

LAIUS gestures dismissal.
SHEPHERD hobbles off towards Delphi.
Pause.

OEDIPUS   I trust my mother is well?

LAIUS   No. She sleeps little and has bad dreams.

OEDIPUS   The Lord Apollo visits her?

LAIUS   She does not talk of her dreams.

OEDIPUS   How old is my mother?

LAIUS   She was nineteen when you were born.

OEDIPUS   And for nineteen years you have kept her from your bed. In her place nineteen years of slim-hipped boys, decked out with pearl bracelets and pretty armour. *Her* boy snatched away the day it was born. No boys for her to kiss and dandle on her knee. An empty bed and the squeals and cries and gurgles of her husband buggering in the next room. Are you surprised she has bad dreams?

LAIUS   The Lord Apollo —

OEDIPUS   Fuck the Lord Apollo. And fuck you. There are such things as daughters. Mothers become quite fond of daughters. Specially if they've had sons whose fathers have nailed their ankles together and flung them out of the house like stinking fish. Bad dreams! I wonder her wits haven't turned and sent her out like the wild women to roam the hills and live on roots and raw flesh.

LAIUS   Don't think it gives me any pleasure waiting here for you to build yourself up into an appropriate passion to murder me. Curse me, curse the Gods: you are cursed yourself. You propose not to kill me but the Oracle does not demand that you kill me wilfully. An accident, perhaps. You trip over a stone. I trip. *(does so; OEDIPUS catches him)* Suppose you had been holding a sword at that moment? You have killed me. Accidentally: but the first prophecy of the Oracle is fulfilled.

OEDIPUS I shall leave at once for Corinth. Or Athens, Argos, Sparta.

LAIUS points towards Delphi. OEDIPUS looks.

What's he doing?

LAIUS Waiting. When he sees me killed he'll lead his sheep back again and raise the alarm. Or has he raised it already? Was that a man moving in the shadow of the trees?

OEDIPUS But if he raises the alarm and I am captured and taken to Thebes I shall be torn to pieces.

LAIUS You are afraid of death?

OEDIPUS Any man who dies before he is fifty has a right to be irritated. No, my point is: that

	fool of a shepherd believes in the Oracle as rigidly as you do. He's not going to gather men to haul me to Thebes and arraign me as your killer. What about the rest of the prophesy? *(shrill voice)* "Lie with your mother and beget children of her!" They won't let the killer of the king marry his widow.
LAIUS	Why not? You will be the redeemer, the saviour of the city. I am not well loved. I can hear the chanting. "Hail Oedipus! Who has delivered us from the tyrant Laius! Hail Oedipus, King of Thebes!" They will carry you on their shoulders through cheering crowds up past the rows of houses and terraced gardens to the palace and there you will see my widow, magnificently dressed in gold and purple. Her arms open to receive you. Arms freshly painted red with the blood of my sleeping-boys. You will be married the same day.

OEDIPUS shakes his head.

You'll have no choice. A good-looking, chunky youth like you — not unlike the man she married. As you say, she's been waiting for a man for nineteen years. You won't have a chance. If you refuse, she will have you drugged and come to your bed then. We can't tell how the prophesy will be fulfilled. All we know is that it will be. If you come upon a boy called Eis, quite young, with the mark of a red heart on his shoulder. If she has not cut his throat or strangled him, let him go free. He was kind. If he is dead, bury him decently.

OEDIPUS Why are you going to Delphi?

LAIUS To consult the Oracle.

OEDIPUS Yes — what for?

LAIUS Concerning a problem I happily bequeath to you. On your way in to Thebes you will pass Mount Phicium. Thebes is rich in hills but Phicium has always been a particular favourite with young men and courting couples. I used to take your mother there. It has shallow caves and streams, glades, groves, shade on a summer day, fine views of the Copaic Lake. But now no one goes there except the very brave or the exceptionally stupid. A monster has come there.

OEDIPUS laughs.

The young men in Thebes also laughed. I wish you joy of your monster.

OEDIPUS   Very well. Tell me of your monster.

LAIUS   What is there to tell? I have not seen her.

OEDIPUS   Her?

LAIUS   So it is said. The head and breasts of a woman, the body of a lion and the wings of an eagle. She arrived one night and made her abode in the mountain. If any young man is unfortunate enough to meet her she asks him a riddle. If he fails to answer it — and no one has yet correctly answered it — she throttles him and tears him to pieces. Before you say it: if no one has met the monster and escaped, how do we know what she does? How indeed! Perhaps some young man's friend hid in the bushes and watched.

OEDIPUS   Which is how it is known what she looks like?

LAIUS   Presumably.

OEDIPUS   Has this young man's friend been questioned?

LAIUS   Even in calm prosperous Corinth you must have rumours that spread everywhere and start from nowhere. Nobody has seen the Sphinx. That may not be her true name. Sphinx, the Strangler. No one has seen her but everyone knows what she looks like. There is another city of Thebes in Egypt. I have heard that in Egypt there is a giant figure carved out of the rock with a human head and the body of a lion. Perhaps some traveller's tale combined with the rumour... All I know is that nearly every morning the strangled, mutilated body of a young Theban is brought down from Mount Phicium. And I have to do — had to do — something about it. It will now be up to you.

OEDIPUS   Always young men?

LAIUS   So it seems.

OEDIPUS   Then go up yourself.

LAIUS   Perhaps it has always been young men because only young men have so far gone up there.

OEDIPUS   Why have they gone up there?

LAIUS   Like you they do not believe in monsters.

OEDIPUS   Then send one of your old men up.

LAIUS   My wife's brother Kreon has been up. He stayed near the summit all night long but reported nothing.

OEDIPUS   And the Sphinx asks a riddle.

LAIUS   So they say.

OEDIPUS   Do they say what riddle she asks? *(LAIUS shakes head)* The young men hiding in the bushes just overhear her say, "What is it that —?" And no more?

LAIUS   Kreon is good at riddles. That's why he volunteered. I haven't the head for them. My wife enjoys them too. She used to have one that went... "What is it that goes on four legs in the morning, two legs in the afternoon and three legs in the evening?"

OEDIPUS   Man.

LAIUS   What?

OEDIPUS   I was asked that riddle only the other day. Back home. *(goes down on all fours, looks up at LAIUS)* Dada. *(stands upright, looks at LAIUS)* Father. *(draws sword, uses it as a stick, leans heavily upon it, limps towards LAIUS)*

LAIUS   Of course. Well. When Jocasta asks you that you'll be able to answer it.

              OEDIPUS plays with his sword. LAIUS looks at it. OEDIPUS at once sheathes it and glances away towards Delphi.

OEDIPUS   If I could understand the purpose of it...

LAIUS   Who are we to question the will of the Gods.

OEDIPUS   Who are they to escape our question? They escape your question. Though when you were younger — to judge by the ache in my feet when the weather is damp — you raised your little voice in a faint ambiguous protest. When you were young, nineteen, twenty years ago, didn't you search your head for the reason this curse was laid upon you? Was my mother loved by Apollo and you stole her from

151

	him? You insulted somebody? Something? Somehow?

LAIUS   I could think of nothing to account for it — then. But I have lived with the curse for twenty years. In that time I have seen unborn sons grow into boys grow into young men. And when I look at what my own son has become I understand the far-seeing purpose of the Gods. In every city the priestly warnings are ignored. Men try to live their lives as if there were no Gods, guided only by themselves. The fate of the house of Laius is to be an example to such men. Through my death and your crime and the shame of our wife men will learn that the Gods are not mocked. Even my faint attempt to resist the Oracle has meaning. Twist we, turn we how we may, our fate hunts us down. We flee from it for twenty years and at the end of our journey all we have done is catch up with it. Therefore worship the gods, obey the Law, attend all the days of your life to the words of the priests.

OEDIPUS I don't like it.

LAIUS   Yes, I pity you. I submit myself to the will of the Gods. You must be forced.

You, the blasphemer, who would like to show the Gods do not exist, you are to be remembered as the man who restored them to greater eminence than before.

OEDIPUS   No. No: look. Things don't happen as neatly as this.

LAIUS   Not in the world you would like but in the world ruled by the Gods.

OEDIPUS   If you want me to kill you to fulfil some divine plan you'll have to convince me it also fulfils some essential human plan. *(turns in the direction of Delphi; waves)* Ahoy, there! *(to LAIUS)* You were right. There are other men there. One with a bow. Apollo?

LAIUS   You think it quite by chance and nothing to do with the Gods that you left Corinth to consult the Oracle?

OEDIPUS   Yes.

LAIUS   And quite by chance and nothing to do with the gods that I left Thebes to consult the Oracle?

OEDIPUS   Why did you?

LAIUS   Chrysippus, my man, wanted to seek out the Sphinx. I could not let him. You think it by chance he wanted to try his luck tonight so that I had to set off here with him today? By chance in time to meet you just before you took the road back to Corinth? By chance at just the time Polyphontes and his sheep came past to confirm the story of your birth?

OEDIPUS   No. Not by chance... Oh! The elegance of it! The subtle... devious... wickedness of it! You're right. Nobody believes in the Gods any more. The altars are neglected. The lion and the lizard keep the courts where Zeus and everyone drank deep. And who loses by this falling away? You'll say "Mankind", of course, but who depends on the gods?

LAIUS   Mankind.

OEDIPUS   Oh, come, come. Depends on the worship of them, the special cuts of sacrificial meat, the regular donations, the one drachma in ten.

LAIUS   The priests.

OEDIPUS   The priests. Well done, father.

LAIUS   Say nothing against the priests.

OEDIPUS   I shan't kill you if you don't let me talk about the priests. If men no longer credit the gods with existence the priests lose their status, their support and, more than that, their point. To lose status is embarrassing, to lose means of support is uncomfortable, but to lose the purpose of one's life leaves a void that must be filled at any cost. Any cost. Your life. My life. His life. *(points towards rock)* What are our lives to set against the return of the people to the altars and the return of purpose to the lives of the priests! And what, as you say, will bring back the people better than an example in the foremost royal house of Greece. Privileged family of princes. If they can defy the Oracle in vain, live in splendour and die in despair — how much less hope have lesser men. Therefore call no man happy till he is dead. Therefore worship the Gods, little men. Obey the priests.

LAIUS   The objections to this story —

OEDIPUS   — can all be answered. *(with a glance towards Delphi)* The priests of Delphi maintain the finest intelligence system in the world. To all intents the only one. Every city in the world keeps a representative there. In its turn the temple sends priests out to every city. Tiresias himself shuffles his way from palace to palace checking on lines of communication and calling recalcitrant kings to order with a smack from his big white stick.

LAIUS puts his hand over OEDIPUS's mouth.
OEDIPUS thrusts it away.

Who told you a son of yours would kill you and marry his mother?

LAIUS The Oracle of Apollo.

OEDIPUS And who told me, vice versa? The Oracle of Apollo.

LAIUS And who told my shepherd to come to this place to meet the Corinthian? Apollo himself!

OEDIPUS In a dream.

LAIUS The Gods can visit us in dreams.

OEDIPUS   The Gods never visit us any time else. The dream is their realm. Who tells us the god Apollo came to the shepherd.

LAIUS   *(after pause)* No, no: he is a shepherd.

OEDIPUS   Why should all the servants of Apollo serve him as priests?

LAIUS   You see enemies everywhere.

OEDIPUS   I was never in danger of my future before. Every incident in our lives has been watched — not by the Gods, as you would have it, but by priests and the agents of priests. Which is very much more alarming. The Gods could be placated by the smoke of burnt offerings but men are inflexible. We have been watched, spied upon, reported on, nudged into action. Deliboeus — he's the one who asked me the riddle about four legs, two legs, three legs — he caused me to go to the Oracle. Zip go the messengers ahead of me and here's your shepherd waiting for me when I arrive. Zip the messages go ahead of me to Delphi and zip back again all the way to Thebes. The plot set in motion twenty years ago is reaching its first climax. The

                    trap begins to close upon King Laius, who
                    finds himself impelled to go to the Oracle.

LAIUS   What are you implying?

OEDIPUS   That you were impelled to meet me here today.

LAIUS   By whom?

OEDIPUS   By whoever impelled you. *(indicates SOLDIER's fallen helmet.)*

                LAIUS strikes him across the mouth.
                OEDIPUS draws his sword, then drops it hastily.

OEDIPUS   I nearly forgot myself. No one we have ever known is beyond suspicion. Least of all those we have wanted to love us.

                LAIUS snatches up the sword, advances on OEDIPUS.
                Take care.

LAIUS   Of what? For what?

                LAIUS forces OEDIPUS back against the rock.

If the Oracle is false, then I am avenging the murder of my man. Traitor or not, he loved me.

LAIUS pricks OEDIPUS with the point of the sword.
OEDIPUS winces.

And if the Oracle is true, nothing was said as to *which* son is destined to kill me. I shall father a second son and keep him in the palace under strict guard. In fifteen years time, when he shows signs of manhood, he will be killed.

LAIUS pricks OEDIPUS again.

Then we'll start a third son. And then a fourth. And when I am sixty or seventy or tired of life, eighty or ninety, as old as Tiresias, then let my fifth or sixth son satisfy the Oracle. But not, little Swollen-foot, not now.

LAIUS prepares to kill OEDIPUS.
Sound of a blind man's white stick tap, tapping.
LAIUS turns his head.
TIRESIAS, blind, walks on from Delphi, led by an ATTENDANT

TIRESIAS   Are we here?

ATTENDANT Yes, master.

OEDIPUS darts away from LAIUS at the rock, picks up LAIUS's sword; stands prepared.

TIRESIAS   Laius son of Labdacus; Oedipus of Corinth.

LAIUS passes his hands across TIRESIAS's face; studies the reaction of his eyes.

Who has taught you to doubt?

LAIUS steps back, confused.

OEDIPUS   You have.

TIRESIAS slowly turns to face OEDIPUS.
You, Tiresias, have taught us doubtful tales and we have learned to laugh at them. And at you. And at Far-Darting Apollo, Lord of the Golden Locks. And at monsters who perch on mountains. And monsters who squat in caves.

LAIUS	*(to TIRESIAS)* Are you deaf as well as blind? Strike him down! The God is deaf!
	An arrow shoots down from the direction of Delphi and strikes the rock. *TIRESIAS and ATTENDANT are unmoved.* *OEDIPUS steps back amazed.* *LAIUS stares at the still quivering arrow, then throws himself to the ground.*
	The God has answered!
OEDIPUS	*(peers in the direction of Delphi)* Of course he hasn't. *(waves)* Well shot, sir!
	OEDIPUS pulls arrow from rock, snaps it in two, drops it on ground; looks at TIRESIAS and laughs, indicating LAIUS.
	Still it impresses him. *(bends over LAIUS)* King Laius?
	LAIUS shakes his head.
	Father?
TIRESIAS	Father?

OEDIPUS   I wasn't supposed to know, was I, till after I'd killed him and married my mother. Then you'd have come tap-tapping along crying, "Unclean! Unclean! Woe unto you, O Thebes, a sinful thing pollutes your soil. Seek him out. Drive him out. Repent. Believe."

TIRESIAS   Why do you call King Laius father? Oedipus son of Polybus.

OEDIPUS   *(staring)* Polybus? *(stares at LAIUS)*

LAIUS stares up at TIRESIAS.

TIRESIAS   Who else should be your father? I remember the day King Polybus came to Delphi. His queen was barren and he sought an heir. The Holy Oracle advised him to lie with the first woman to greet him on his way home to Corinth for she would bear him a son. And so it befell.

OEDIPUS   Who was she?

TIRESIAS remains silent.

LAIUS   She is Jocasta. *(stands)* Polybus visited us on his return from Delphi. My wife greeted him outside the Neistian Gate.

That night he told me she was the first woman he had seen or spoken to since he left the Holy Oracle. What the Holy Oracle had told him he did not reveal. My wife! In my own house!

TIRESIAS   By the will of Apollo.

OEDIPUS   Wait. The baby born to Jocasta, my mother, was not his.

OEDIPUS points to LAIUS. TIRESIAS shakes head.
OEDIPUS observes this, passes his hands across TIRESIAS's face, keeps his eyes fixed on TIRESIAS's eyes.

King Laius exposed the son of King Polybus, who is my father.

TIRESIAS nods.

Who I am destined, says the Oracle, to kill and return to marry — his queen. *(points to LAIUS)* My mother.

TIRESIAS neither shakes his head nor nods.
OEDIPUS clicks his fingers to attract his attention.

TIRESIAS   You left the Sacred Close of Apollo in great haste. The Holy Oracle speaks in riddles. Through her mouth the God says such a thing; and means such a thing; but what is that thing is for priests to unriddle. Without priests the words of the God must be misunderstood, distorted, set awry. A king of, as it might be, Lydia... King Croesus of Lydia comes to Delphi to ask if he should invade the kingdom of Persia. He is told that if he attacks the Persians he will destroy a mighty empire. Joyfully he returns to Lydia, he leads his army across the Persian frontier, and he is totally defeated. Because he did not ask of the priests which empire would be destroyed.

OEDIPUS   And so?

TIRESIAS   Father... Mother... *(to ATTENDANT)* What would you say, boy?

ATTENDANT   Well, one could argue, I think, that in a certain circumstance, yes, one's mother could be considered to be the wife of one's father.

TIRESIAS   Oedipus son of Polybus.

OEDIPUS   I marry Queen Merope? Why?

ATTENDANT   I would be right in thinking, would I not, that if the King of Corinth dies you will reign in his stead? It could be desirable to wed his queen also. The alliance with Attica, you understand. A political marriage, naturally. There are precedents.

OEDIPUS   Are there precedents for a woman barren twenty years bearing children?

ATTENDANT   Oh, yes. Queen Alcyone of Elis after twenty years was brought to bed of Pylenor. And the Queen of Euboea last year after twenty-five years and four husbands — and many other men, I greatly fear — was at long last blessed with twins.

LAIUS snatches up a sword (OEDIPUS's)

LAIUS   And father's? What's the priestly line regarding fathers?

ATTENDANT   Well, yes, in certain circumstances, once again, one could maintain that, for certain purposes, one's father is the husband of one's mother. Hephaistos was acknowledged as the father of —

OEDIPUS   For certain purposes. What do you suppose those are, father?

TIRESIAS   Father but yet not father.

OEDIPUS   *(to LAIUS)* You see what they want us to do? Whichever way you look at it, they have fixed on the house of Laius. If I am your son, they want me to kill you. If I am Polybus's son, they still want me to kill you. The only fact to stay clear in the cloudy waters of their interpretation is that Jocasta is my mother. But no doubt after you've been killed they'll put forward another story that shows she isn't my mother after all, not at all, oh, it's quite safe to marry her, safest of all, indeed, politically desirable too, the Boeotian alliance. And after a year or two: tap tap tap and the story will change again. It's not that I object to being sacrificed. I would prefer it to happen to somebody else. But I've learned enough about government, even in sleepy-time Corinth, to know that the people require an occasional calamity to strike somebody down. It binds the survivors together, tethers them. A careful succession of catastrophes acts as a most valuable cement. I would be ready to sacrifice myself to cement a city. But not to patch up an idol.

LAIUS I don't know whose son you are but you are a fool. The purpose of cementing a city is to get the blocks of stone to keep in their place. The function of cement in a community is identical. Nothing is so effective in making people keep to their own little allotted places as getting a God to rule over them. The King reigns in the name of the God; the priests serve in the name of the God. The people serve the King, the priests, and stay where they are put. If it is good for Thebes that I must die then it is desirable that I die. If it is good also for Athens and Corinth, Argos and Sparta, for Egypt, Persia, Rome, then I am honoured that upon me the lot has fallen. And if the Gods are fictions, and you and I are to patch up a row of marble idols, that patching will cement a whole world.

LAIUS casts away his sword, bares breast for OEDIPUS to kill him.

TIRESIAS King Laius, in the Temple of Apollo your name shall be recorded as a true servant of the God.

OEDIPUS   Or the idol.

TIRESIAS   Of order.

OEDIPUS   My name, I think, will not be recorded there. You can lead an armed man to your victim but you cannot make him strike.

TIRESIAS   Indeed not. Evidently a miscalculation has been made. But it should not be beyond our wits to rectify it.

TIRESIAS raises hand, clicks fingers. LAIUS and OEDIPUS turn and look towards Delphi.

This drama has been worked upon for over twenty years. Discussion was begun several years earlier. Predictions were plotted, accidents considered, alternative actors prepared. Your mantle and tunic, please.

ATTENDANT steps forward to OEDIPUS.

Also your shoes. The buckle given to you by Queen Merope. Belt and sword.

ATTENDANT removes his own priestly tunic and stands naked or in loin-cloth, removes sandals, indicates his feet to OEDIPUS.

ATTENDANT Sufficiently swollen. An abnormal enlargement of the heel bone inherited from my mother. But it will serve when the shepherd comes to the palace to identify me as Oedipus son of Laius.

LAIUS *(to OEDIPUS)* Come along, boy.

ATTENDANT picks up sword (OEDIPUS's), examines bloodstains.

His body is behind the rock. Will you see it is buried.
ATTENDANT nods, handles sword.

OEDIPUS I am curious as to my future.

ATTENDANT holds out his tunic to him.

I can't adapt to guiding blind old men about Greece. There is nothing for me to do. In Thebes. Or in Corinth.

LAIUS You should have gone when I told you and found some remote place beyond the seas where no one has ever heard of Delphi, still less of Thebes.

OEDIPUS *(to ATTENDANT)* Oedipus..? *(ATTENDANT smiles)* What happens when — Deliboeus comes from Corinth to attend your coronation as King of Thebes?

ATTENDANT He will recognise me as his childhood comrade. *(OEDIPUS nods slowly)* He will return home to tell King Polybus and Queen Merope of their son's good fortune.

OEDIPUS Their son?

ATTENDANT Their son; his son *(LAIUS)*; his son *(TIRESIAS)*.
ATTENDANT knocks the sword (LAIUS's) from OEDIPUS's hand.
OEDIPUS starts back.
ATTENDANT holds out his other hand for OEDIPUS's clothes.
OEDIPUS undresses, passes his clothes to ATTENDANT who dresses in them.

OEDIPUS Naked, without a name, I came into this world. Naked, unnamed, I shall go out of it.

SHEPHERD walks on from Delphi. He shows none of his former frailty. He carries a bow and quiver of arrows.

LAIUS May I be told how I shall go out of it? What is your name, boy?

ATTENDANT Oedipus.

LAIUS As you will.

TIRESIAS Oedipus on his way from Delphi has met you on your way to Delphi. Here. Your soldier has ordered him to step off the road to make way for your chariot. Oedipus refuses. Your soldier fights him and is killed. You strike at Oedipus.

ATTENDANT slashes his arm with his sword, leaving a line of blood.

Not knowing who you are, he pulls you out of your chariot, your feet are caught in the reins, he whips up the horses and they drag you to death.

LAIUS *(after pause)* A nasty death,

TIRESIAS You might prefer to be stunned beforehand.

LAIUS Yes.

SHEPHERD, unnoticed behind LAIUS, delivers a rabbit punch to his neck. LAIUS drops to the ground. SHEPHERD lifts up the body.

TIRESIAS Loop the reins twice round each ankle.

SHEPHERD carries off LAIUS's unconscious body beyond the rock.
OEDIPUS stares after him.
ATTENDANT makes finishing adjustments to his mantle.
TIRESIAS takes a scroll from inside his tunic and reads.
He is not blind.
Sudden loud noise of horses goaded. Neighing in frenzy, rearing and galloping, dragging a chariot.
Sound fades into the distance.
From behind the rock comes the SHEPHERD, now bearing the body of the SOLDIER.

Ah, yes. *(to OEDIPUS)* Where did you fight?

OEDIPUS is silent.

ATTENDANT   There is blood here, on the sand. *(points to where OEDIPUS and SOLDIER fought)*

TIRESIAS   *(looking)* Good. *(to SHEPHERD)* There.

SHEPHERD places SOLDIER's body down as he lay when OEDIPUS killed him.

(to ATTENDANT) You can be off now. You should be near Thebes tomorrow evening. When you have answered the Sphinx's riddle, pick up her lionskin and take it with you as proof of your victory. The Queen is a handsome woman, frantic for motherhood, and you should find her amply passionate. You should rule for about six, seven years. I'll instruct you later on the business of the blinding. Good fortune.

ATTENDANT   Thank you, master.

ATTENDANT walks off towards Thebes.

OEDIPUS   I am starting to feel irrelevant.

TIRESIAS   It became apparent some time ago that you were likely to prove useless to our purpose. A man of intelligence was required but a man with blind spots to his intelligence. A man capable of grasping all the relevant details, except one: the one that rivets the others into their true position. Unfortunately, you have not only wanted to know all the answers: you have wanted to know all the questions. If a question is asked in its proper form the answer is contained within it. Every problem becomes a solution. In other circumstances, in other times, an admirable situation: but not here and now. Your death is our loss but it is a loss we must bear. And should bear. Society is too raw for your questions. You disturb the very delicate balance of this world. Here and now the Gods are necessary and the priesthood is necessary and you are not necessary.

OEDIPUS   Suppose I became a priest of Apollo?

TIRESIAS What would you do?

OEDIPUS   Wreck Delphi within a year.

TIRESIAS Exactly. In the Temple of Apollo stands the omphalos, the navel stone of the world.

OEDIPUS	I saw it. A white marble stone patterned all over like a pine cone.
TIRESIAS	That is the version the public sees. The true omphalos is not on show, not showy, nothing particular to look at, nothing apparently to distinguish it from a thousand other stones you could pick up in a day's climb on Parnassus. But is the navel, umbo, middle, central boss of the world. Wreck Delphi and the world falls.

SHEPHERD takes a pace towards OEDIPUS who steps back and trips over the outstretched white stick of TIRESIAS. OEDIPUS falls to the ground.

OEDIPUS	No escape? *(to TIRESIAS)* If you were blind I would try. *(to SHEPHERD)* What does anger me is the thought of you tottering along to Thebes in six or seven years and looking at King — Oedipus's feet and saying, "Yes, I drew the cruel rivets from those feet myself." Nineteen years ago you preserved my life. Now you end it. What can I do?

OEDIPUS has gathered sand in each hand: he flings one handful into SHEPHERD's face, the other handful into TIRESIAS's face. He springs to his feet, darts between the temporarily blinded TIRESIAS and SHEPHERD, and runs off along the road to Corinth.

TIRESIAS and SHEPHERD stumble helplessly, rubbing their eyes.

TIRESIAS recovers his sight first, peers about, sees the retreating OEDIPUS on the Corinth road.

TIRESIAS *(to SHEPHERD)* Shoot him!

SHEPHERD gropes for his bow, draws an arrow, shoots it after OEDIPUS.
TIRESIAS and SHEPHERD, squinting, follow its flight.

Again.

SHEPHERD shoots another arrow.
Again they follow its flight.

Go after him.

SHEPHERD stumbles over SOLDIER's body, recovers his balance, hurries after OEDIPUS, already drawing his bow again.

TIRESIAS prepares to follow him, checks himself, inspects the scene, picks up the two fragments of the first arrow, picks up his scroll, unrolls and reads from it.

Oedipus meets Laius where three roads cross. *(marks this entry with arrow tip)* Death of soldier. *(marks)* Death of Laius. *(marks)* Oedipus to Thebes. *(marks, stares in direction of Thebes; he unrolls scroll further, reading entries)* Sphinx... Jocasta... Plagues... Kreon to Delphi — an unclean thing... Tiresias to Thebes — unclean thing... Recall of the shepherd... The Corinthian... The Fall of Oedipus. And with the Fall of Oedipus the return of the people to the gods, the return of order to the land. Balance. Know thyself but — nothing too much. With the Fall of Oedipus...

He looks along the Corinth road, frowns, calls:

Cut him off against the cliff!

He watches.

Yes!

He watches.

Yes.

He pulls on the handle of his white stick which reveals itself to be a swordstick. He takes a last look around.

Yes.

Grasping his weapon TIRESIAS strides after the SHEPHERD and OEDIPUS along the Corinth road.

SOLDIER, dead, alone on the stage.

Black.